Through the Gospel with Dom Helder Camara

Through the Gospel with Dom Helder Camara

Translated by
Alan Neame

ORBIS BOOKS

Maryknoll, New York 10545

The Catholic Foreign Mission Society of America (Maryknoll) recruits and trains people for overseas missionary service. Through Orbis Books Maryknoll aims to foster the international dialogue that is essential to mission. The books published, however, reflect the opinions of their authors and are not meant to represent the official position of the society.

Originally published in French by Editions du Seuil, 1985
English translation © 1986 by Darton, Longman and Todd Ltd
Published in Great Britain by Darton, Longman and Todd Ltd

Darton, Longman and Todd Ltd ISBN 0 232 51685 5

Published in 1986 in the United States of America by Orbis Books, Maryknoll, NY 10545
Orbis ISBN 0-88344-266-3

Contents

Acknowledgement

Scriptural quotations are taken, with the occasional alteration, from the New Jerusalem Bible © 1985 Darton, Longman and Todd Ltd and Doubleday and Company Inc. and reproduced by permission of the publishers.

Introduction

Dear Dom Helder,

It was due to you, between two sessions of the Second Vatican Council, that a large number of western bishops and several journalists (myself included) learned of the existence of a 'third world', a universe of hunger in which 'houses weren't houses and people weren't people any more'. We were made aware of such a monstrous imbalance of resources, of such an imbalance between wealth and aspiration, as might well lead to worldwide disaster.

Should I say, 'Due to you' or 'Thanks to you'?

That earliest image still remains: the scene a rather rococo reception room in a big hotel in Rome. John XXIII having broken with the tradition that the pope should be a distant, hieratic, silent figure, and the Church — that largest of world communities — having boldly undertaken the course of re-examining its role in a topsy-turvy world, the bishops, Council Fathers and their advisers now felt free to speak their minds.

Dom Helder, I don't need to remind you how newspaper, radio and television journalists are always on the lookout for something new. . . Radio Luxemburg, as it was then still called, had organised two question-and-answer evenings on the *schemas* of the Council, under the chairmanship of a priest called Father Emile Gabel of whom you, José de Broucker and I were very fond. You were present with those two remarkable and capable men Monsignor Rodhain and Father Lebret. You came to speak on the schema: The Church of the Poor. On the previous evening at our first live broadcast, I had been given a tactful warning by one of our guests, Mgr Garrone the then Archbishop of Toulouse: 'You have given us a wonderful reception, the dinner before we went on the

1

air was delicious, we are truly touched by the way you've entertained us, but I'm told that tomorrow you've got Dom Helder Camara coming. How do you think he'll react to this VIP treatment? You realize, the Church of the Poor is no mere form of words for him.'

Consequently, dear Dom Helder, we awaited your arrival with some trepidation. The first thing I did was to offer you our apologies: 'You are doing us a great honour by taking part in this programme, so we thought we ought to entertain you as well as we possibly could. I sincerely hope you won't be offended.' That was the first occasion you ever patted my hand and squeezed my arm, as they do in Brazil. And this and the expression on your face were more reassuring than whatever it was you said.

You quietly took your place at table; you nibbled at your food in what I didn't know then was your usual way. With the Council Fathers present, we journalists were speculating on the type of question likely to be put in connection with this or that schema. It so chanced that 'The Church of the Poor' came under discussion just as we reached the dessert; white-gloved waiters were sticking sparklers into the *omelettes norvégiennes*. Everyone looked at you. You spoke – do you remember? 'Forgive me if I seem a trifle bemused. . . The country I come from is so utterly different, it might be on another planet. . .' You spoke for twenty minutes, no one said a word and the waiters, not daring to move, stood spellbound, the ice melting and the snow-laid eggs collapsing on the silver platters in their hands.

Later, in front of the microphones, you were just the same: just as passionate, just as tenderly vehement, just as overwhelming. You talked about the poor in Brazil, you talked to your French-speaking listeners, you talked to us journalists who are often called scavengers or worse – all with the same respect, consideration and love.

That night a project was born. The power that drives this man is drawn from the words and deeds of Jesus of Nazareth. These words and deeds are revealed to us in the gospels. Why not make a TV 'serial unlike any other', a series of programmes to consist of individual gospel texts taken in chronological order from the life of Christ, and ask Dom

Helder to comment on and relate each episode to the modern world?

With this in mind and thanks to that 'man of the media' Jacques Antoine, who believed in the idea because he believed in you, my wife and I came to visit you fifteen years later in Recife. There we saw your poor people for ourselves: the devotion, affection and real faith you inspire in those around you. The sneers and strictures too in certain quarters. For three or four hours each day you would come and sit in the parlour of some nuns you had asked to put us up. We would read a passage aloud. You would sit quite still listening with your eyes shut. Then after a moment's silence you would open your eyes and, with your hands raised in a gesture we soon came to know well, begin to speak. Oblivious of the mike and video-recorder, Dom Helder talked about and – I think – often with the Lord.

From the recordings we made then, José de Broucker and your other friends at Seuil have now produced this book. And I hope everyone who reads your words in print will be as enthralled and moved as I was, when I listened to 'you in that shadowy convent parlour in Recife and heard, if you will pardon the expression, 'the Gospel according to Dom Helder'.

ROGER BOURGEON

1

R. B.: *What's the point of talking about Jesus today?*

D. H.: Because this Man changed history. He is alive in history. At every step I meet him every day. And I meet him in the flesh. He said, whoever is suffering, humiliated, crushed is he. In our own times when more than two-thirds of the human race are living in sub-human conditions, it's easy enough to meet him in the flesh.

Was Jesus exactly as the evangelists say he was? I'm no biblical critic. I'm not against biblical criticism, but I prefer to let the critics get on with their own discussions. For my part I am as sure of Christ's existence as I am of my own hand with its five fingers I can touch and see. I meet Jesus every day. And we are one. No doubt about it.

But was there any particular moment when you discovered this?

Like a child discovering it has feet. It's always known it's got feet, but one day it discovers them.

At a given moment, certainly, I became aware of Christ's presence in those who suffer, and of his presence inside myself. When? I don't know.

I was brought up in a family that was Christian not so much by label as in actions. My father and mother didn't practise their religion very regularly. Who gave me the idea of becoming a priest when I was still a little boy? What did this desire amount to in my childish mind?

Anyhow, one day my father asked me this question: 'You keep saying you want to be a priest. But do you really understand what being a priest involves?' He then sketched the

5

ideal priest in terms exactly corresponding to what I felt without understanding, to what I dreamed though unable to put it into words: 'My boy, priest and self-centredness don't go together. That's impossible. A priest isn't his own master. He has only one reason for living: to live for others.'

This corresponded precisely to what the Lord had already sown in my heart. All my life I've lived the dream of being one with Christ to help my fellow-beings conquer their self-centredness.

You speak to Jesus. Does he speak to you?

Christ speaks to all of us. He is here.

But do you hear him speaking?

Whenever you listen to someone who is suffering, you hear Christ's voice. And whenever you meet someone suffering, you meet him in person.

In one of your books you say that every night, during your 'vigil' as you call it, you talk to Jesus. . .

There's no need to talk; thinking is enough. During my 'vigil' I try to recover unity with Christ. And with him I relive the meetings of the past day. I think, for instance, about the mother who told me about the problems she has with her husband, with her children, and how hard she finds it to feed them. And, through this very real mother whom I know by name, I think about all the mothers throughout the world throughout the ages: the poor ones, the rich ones, the happy ones, the unhappy ones. Or I think about the man I saw working in the street, emptying dustbins. I had caught his eye. He didn't dare offer me his hand. I virtually had to force him: 'Work isn't what soils our hands, friend. No hand was ever soiled by work. Self-centredness is what soils them.' This man, Francisco or Antonio as he may be, reminds me of working men throughout the world throughout the ages. Then I say to Christ our brother, 'Lord, two thousand years

6

after your death injustices are growing worse and worse.'
Reviewing the day like this, I find time passes very quickly.

*Do you feel this presence of Jesus constantly within you? Or are
there absences, silences, gaps from time to time?*

Occasionally on receiving a small favour, one might be
tempted to think of it as one's due. But when the favour is
an enormous one, it's harder to imagine one might have
deserved it; one can't be tempted to vanity then.

I say this in connection with the favour the Lord has done
me of always being so immediately present in me, in us, in
our neighbour in a general sense, but most particularly in
those who suffer. So present that very often when I'm thinking
ahead to encounters which, were I on my own, I should find
worrying, tiring or irritating, as for instance when I have to
advise someone or tell someone off, I say, 'Lord, be one with
me. Listen with my ears, look through my eyes, speak by my
lips. I don't know what to say. Speak. I lend you my lips.
Let my presence be your presence, Lord.' That's what I do.

At Rio, right on the top of Mount Corcovado, stands a vast
statue of Christ. Very often it's hidden in the clouds, and I
think, 'Lord, some of our brothers and sisters are suffering so
frightfully, they think you have vanished from their lives, that
you're hiding, that you aren't there any more. I know you're
there, but they can't discover you anywhere.'

When I consider the enormous responsibility entailed in
always seeing the unclouded Christ, I can't impute this to
any merit or righteousness of my own. Then I pray for those
who are in the fog and can't see anything: 'Don't you worry,
Christ is there. These are only clouds, but he's there all the
same. The clouds will go away, and then you will see for
yourselves, the Lord is there.'

*Doesn't it sometimes strike you as odd that, in taking human form,
God should have chosen an insignificant nation like the Jews?*

Not at all, I think it's marvellous. Christ came for all people
of all times. But he found the best way of being present
everywhere was to choose one particular spot in the world, a

7

certain culture, a specific language. This is an important lesson for all those of us who are charged with perpetuating the living presence of Christ. We haven't been created to exist in a vacuum. Oh no! We've been created to be incarnate in some corner of the world, in which we've been put or to which we are led by the will of God.

Here in Brazil I meet missionaries from almost every country in the world: priests, religious, members of the laity. They come to us in the spirit of the incarnation. They assume our culture, they speak our language. They merge so thoroughly with our people, they become our brothers and sisters. They take on all our own problems. Not to solve them, but to encourage us to do so. Through them, through all of us together, the incarnation goes on, and so does the redemption.

By many of us Christians, before the Second Vatican Council, the Jews were looked on as deicides.

I never can understand this hatred for the Jews. They and we belong to the same family. The God of Abraham, Isaac and Jacob is our God. Mary the mother of Christ was a Jewess. It is utter hypocrisy to blame our Jewish brothers for Christ's death. If Christ died, this was because of our weaknesses, our sins. We are all deicides.

But happily the dead Christ rose again. This is what matters to me: Christ's resurrection. We are children of the resurrection. We are born not to die but to rise again. And I even manage to forget we are deicides – since I believe that, even if we had never sinned, the Son of God would still have found some means or other of becoming human, to share more closely in our human nature, even to death.

God has a weakness for human beings. God loves the whole creation but, in the creation, has an especially tender spot for us. This love between God and human beings is fantastic. Even if we hadn't sinned, I am convinced God would have found some good reason for becoming incarnate. He would have taken human nature, to teach us how to share in his divine nature.

It's wonderful what God did in creating human beings. We have much in common with minerals, with stones. We also have much in common with vegetables. Trees breathe, feed, grow; so do we. We are clearly brothers and sisters to the animals. Above us, we share in the nature of the angels and we also share in the nature of God. . . What an adventure, what a daring thing, to assemble so many differing characteristics in one creature! That's why we find it so hard to strike a balance: there are so many worlds tugging at us inside. It is Christ who gives us unity. Christ unites all those worlds that exist inside us.

In that case do you think humankind is unique as a species in the universe?

I think it would be completely absurd to suppose that there is life only on earth, when there are millions and millions of other planets. When speaking of the Creator's preference for humanity, I'm only talking about our own little earth. I don't know what goes on elsewhere in the universe. But one day we shall know.

I remember when the first astronauts went to the moon, I ran into very simple people who refused to believe it. 'It's United States propaganda,' they said. 'No, it isn't. Not this time. Human beings have really got to the moon!' – 'Why then, it's an insult to God. We've really gone too far.' – 'No, we haven't, brother. Don't be alarmed. This is only the beginning of the beginning. It won't be long before we get to Saturn – and we shall get there – and then we shall see we haven't reached the end, the limits of the universe, but only the end of the beginning.'

If there really are other forms of life, do you think they know about God and know Jesus?

When I think of all those different worlds united in the human creature here on earth, I feel myself to be brother to each of them. Joyfully I lend my voice to the stones, the trees, the animals in my street and those in the forest. And I say: Perhaps you don't know how to talk or think. Perhaps you don't know there's a Creator. So I shall speak for you. I'm lending you my voice.

By the same token I think, if there are millions of creatures that perhaps have never heard the name of Christ, yet Christ is with them nonetheless. Christ is everywhere, with God's entire creation, and not merely with those who know him. The only difference between Christians who do know Christ and the others who don't is that we have greater responsibilities.

In his book The Hidden Years of Christ, *Robert Aron says that Moses was the instrument by which God triumphed over the primitive idolatry of the Israelites, and that Jesus was the instrument by which he triumphed over the sophisticated idolatry of the Greeks and Romans. What is needed today to conquer materialism as a philosophy? Aron didn't name an instrument for doing this.*

Materialism? What do you mean by that? I see matter as something living. In its own way it speaks, it sings, it prays. And it is holy, since everything that exists has either been created directly by the Lord or has been created by the Creator working through the co-creator, the human race.

How well I understand Teilhard de Chardin when he dives into the heart of the matter and discovers it to be alive!

So you see no frontiers between matter, life and spirit?

No, no frontier. I find it is just as easy to pray to the Lord when I'm looking at a child smiling, or the sun rising, or a jet passing overhead. Because these are all part of creation.

2

The angel Gabriel was sent by God to a town called Nazareth, to a virgin betrothed to a man named Joseph, of the House of David; and the virgin's name was Mary. . . And the angel said to her, 'Mary, do not be afraid; you have won God's favour. Look! You are to conceive in your womb and bear a son, and you must name him Jesus.' (Luke 1:26–31)

St Matthew tells how an 'angel of the Lord' appeared to Joseph in a dream and said, 'Joseph son of David, do not be afraid to take Mary home as your wife, since she has conceived what is in her by the Holy Spirit. . .' (Matt. 1:20). Dom Helder, as regards this series of angelic apparitions, do you think people can believe in this sort of thing today? Do you believe in angels yourself?

I can well imagine many people find it hard to believe in angels. But I don't find it difficult at all. In the created world I see minerals, vegetables, animals, humanity. And between humanity and God, it seems to me, there is room for creatures which are our brothers and sisters as regards the spirit but do not have heavy bodies like ours.

I am on such familiar terms with my brothers the angels and am so convinced the Lord helps the human race by means of angels that I have given my own angel a name. It's not his proper name – at the moment I don't know what his real name is – but it makes him more real to me. I have given him the name my mother used to call me when she was very pleased with me. 'Keep it up, José!' she would say. That's the name I have given my angel. And I can already imagine how happy I shall be when, having reached the Father's house, I meet my angel in it and hear him tell me what his real name is.

You are all entitled to smile at me and my simplicity. But I can tell you this: travelling along with José my angel keeps me going, keeps my spirits up.

Naturally I don't keep praying to my angel all the time over every petty problem. But in those most difficult, most critical moments, when there is no more human help to be had, then I ask my angel to protect me: 'José, José, I know you're always there to help me. Help me! Better still, help me to help!' Never has he failed me. Never.

It's funny. I must confess I've never seen an angel. Not even my own angel. But that he's present is absolutely clear to me. I'm absolutely convinced he is.

One time in Rome, just once. . . This was during the Holy Year in 1950. In those days we didn't yet have concelebration in the Western Church. Each priest had to say 'his own' mass. We used to queue up to say mass. This particular day I arrived early at one of the churches in Rome to say mass. But I couldn't see where to stand so as to get to the head of the queue. Some fellow-priest was always slipping in ahead of me. By this time it was almost midday. There was a good Franciscan brother there, getting the altar ready and serving each mass. When he thought he'd finished with the last priest, he suddenly noticed I was still waiting my turn. Thinking you've already finished and then finding out that you haven't, can make you cross. It made him cross. So I said, 'Never mind, Brother, I'll come tomorrow. The Lord has seen I intended saying mass today. I'll say it tomorrow.' – 'No, no, no!' he said. And he got the altar ready. However, he kept one question up his sleeve: 'Who, may I ask, is going to serve your mass?' There always had to be someone else there besides the priest. 'Don't worry. My angel will serve the mass.' 'My angel?' . . . Whereupon . . . I can't explain it. Perhaps it was something to do with the electricity. There was such a brilliant light in the church that the poor Franciscan fell on his knees. He wept, he trembled, he trembled, he wept. I didn't want him to stay and serve my mass. But he did stay, trembling like a leaf and weeping right through the service.

12

Some people, because they don't believe in miracles, produce such complicated explanations that these are more supernatural than the supernatural itself.

The virginity and assumption of Mary for example: do these raise any problem for you?

I believe that overriding the laws of nature presents no problem to God. But in any case we see light pass through glass without breaking it. Were I the Son of God, I should do far greater marvels than those for my mother.

Even so, isn't there a certain excessiveness, an element of superstition in much Marian devotion?

Where will you not find superstition? I know plenty of educated people who laugh at the rosary, processions, devotions to the Virgin, but who still won't set foot outside the house before knowing whether the day is lucky for business affairs . . . or for love. Who refuse to get out at the thirteenth floor. . . How silly! Of the two, I prefer my own people's simplicity.

Here and there, I grant you, there may perhaps be stronger devotion to Mary than to Christ. Mary's greatness lies in being Christ's mother. But Christ, and Christ alone, is our Redeemer.

What about apparitions of the Virgin? Why should there be apparitions?

Why not? Why shouldn't the Blessed Virgin, Christ's mother and our mother, mother of all graces and mother of sinners; why shouldn't she appear to bring comfort, encouragement and help? Why not?

I know that may sound naive. But when I look at all these educated people and all these trendy youngsters who would really like to pray but don't know how, and are into every kind of mystery religion, every sort of initiation rite, every brand of cult imported from the East and elsewhere. . .

3

So Joseph set out from the town of Nazareth in Galilee for Judaea, to David's town called Bethlehem, since he was of David's house and line, in order to be registered together with Mary, his betrothed, who was with child. Now it happened that, while they were there, the time came for her to have her child, and she gave birth to a son, her first-born. She wrapped him in swaddling clothes and laid him in a manger because there was no room for them in the living space. (Luke 2:4-7)

One can't help being moved by this story whenever one hears it. It's Christmastime now, Dom Helder. Have there been any Christmasses that have had a marked effect on your life?

In parts of the world like ours, you know, we can live this scene for ourselves almost every day. Because we are actually living through the 'drama of the land'. Big companies buy up acres of land in the country's interior and families that have lived there for years and years are then obliged to leave. When they arrive in the cities, Recife for instance, they look for somewhere to live. Often the wife is pregnant. They end up by building miserable hovels – you might say sub-hovels – where no one else wants to live, nearly always in the swamps. And there Christ is born. There is no ox or donkey, but there is a pig – pigs and chickens sometimes. That's the crib, the living crib. . .

At Christmas, naturally, I celebrate mass in various churches. But I also like to say mass in one of these living cribs.

Why should I go on pilgrimage to Bethlehem, to the historic

birthplace of Christ, when I see Christ being born here, physically, every moment of the day? He's called Joao, Francisco, Antonio, Sebastiao, Severino. . . But he is the Christ.

Oh, how blind we are, how deaf we are! How hard it is to grasp that the Gospel is still going on.

4

Now in Jerusalem there was a man named Simeon. He was an upright and devout man; he looked forward to the restoration of Israel and the Holy Spirit rested on him. It had been revealed to him by the Holy Spirit that he would not see death until he had set eyes on the Christ of the Lord. Prompted by the Spirit he came to the Temple; and when the parents brought in the child Jesus to do for him what the Law required, he took him into his arms and blessed God; and he said: 'Now, Master, you can let your servant go in peace, as you promised; for my eyes have seen your salvation. . .'

As the child's father and mother were wondering at the things that were being said about him, Simeon blessed them and said to Mary his mother, 'Look, he is destined for the fall and for the rise of many in Israel, destined to be a sign that is opposed – and a sword will pierce your soul too – so that the secret thoughts of many may be laid bare.' (Luke 2:25–35)

Everything the Scriptures foretold about the sufferings of Christ, everything Christ himself foretold about the sufferings to be endured by those who follow him, is more than easy to grasp: such are the tangible facts of life as we ourselves experience them.

Simeon's words can be repeated to any mother, particularly among the poor. Children are their riches – which is why I'm opposed to any contraceptive programme manipulated by people who don't want to see the poor multiply. Equally, however, children are their sorrow.

16

When a mother's milk runs dry because she's under-nourished, when she can't squeeze another drop of milk from her breast because there isn't any, when hunger becomes chronic from birth to the age of three or four, her child is damaged for life.

Seeing these living cribs wherever you go, do you approve of traditional Christmas cribs, which were in a sense invented by St Francis of Assisi when he used to encourage the villagers to join in re-enacting the adoration of the shepherds round the Child of Bethlehem?

In our part of the world the poor love dramatizations. These aren't shows or theatrical performances. It is the way children behave.

When a child climbs on a chair and imitates an aeroplane, he actually is an aeroplane. He takes off. The engine roars. He flies through the clouds. He flies over deserts and seas. How dim-witted you would have to be, not to see he really is an aeroplane.

One day I was walking back through a *favella*. A little boy came running along with his arms out wide. I nearly got in his way. I apologized: 'So sorry! I didn't see your car coming.' He looked at me with ineffable contempt: 'My car? This is a space-ship!' He was navigating among the stars.

So when people here enact scenes from the Gospel, they aren't acting at all. They are really living these scenes. The Gospel is something alive. When Christ heals the blind, the deaf, the dumb, the paralytics, when he sets about resurrecting a child or an old friend, when he talks to the woman of Samaria, this is something very close to them.

It's the same with the crib. Instead of making a lovely artificial crib, they make a cradle out of an old packing case or an old petrol can – as the poor do – and lay it down among the pigs. It sometimes happens, when mothers have to go out to work, that when they come home they find the pigs have eaten the baby. Naturally they do what they can to make a corner safe somewhere but accidents will happen. Isn't that terrible?

This is how people find out what it was like for Christ to

17

be born among the beasts. Children are still being born in the mud among the pigs today.

In that case, Dom Helder, aren't you shocked at the way Christmas is celebrated in wealthy European countries with all those meals and presents?

I find it hard to judge. And in any case we haven't the right to judge. It's hard to understand the thought-processes of someone who has been born and always lived in a wealthy country, in comfort and even more than comfort. Just as it would be hard for such a person to understand what it's like to live in sub-human conditions. You have to see it, you have to experience it, to understand it.

I think our responsibility, our task, is to awaken people's consciences. Starting with the consciences of the rich people in our own country. We ought to do what in the past we have all too often forgotten to do, as regards the children of the rich who attend our schools and colleges, as regards the wives of the rich who attend mass at least on Sunday, and even the rich men themselves who come to church at Christmas, Easter and for weddings and funerals. This is what we ought to say to them: 'It's all right for you to think about your children, your homes, your businesses. But we are all brothers and sisters, we all have the same Father. What is not all right in a self-styled Christian country is for one per cent to be too rich, five per cent to be very rich, and ten per cent to be rich, while the mass of the poor and the too-poor make up the remainder.'

The other thing we have to do is raise the level of awareness in the wealthy countries. And there, fortunately, the Lord is awakening awakeners. There are more and more groups, mainly of young people, urging, forcing people to take notice, by demonstrating how, if the wealthy countries are growing wealthier and wealthier and the poor countries are growing poorer and poorer, this isn't a matter of race or brains or guts; it's due to grave injustices.

If indeed there are families today for whom celebrating Christmas means spending lots of money while practically forgetting about Christ and certainly forgetting all about the poor, I also know there are more and more people whose consciences are aroused at Christmastime.

I know there is a great deal to be done. But the Spirit of God has already begun the work, and many sensitive, sincere young people are carrying it forward and will complete it.

What about the Church: its huge cathedrals, grand ceremonies, embroidery, gold, music? Is this the true spirit of Christmas? The Church has begun reducing some of this. Some people say: too much; others: not enough.

The Curé d'Ars, whom I deeply love, used to make this distinction: for himself, nothing or virtually nothing; but for the Lord, no limit to the out-lay. For a ciborium or a monstrance, expense was no object.

For many centuries we too made it our concern to build fine churches, very rich ones sometimes, big schools, big hospitals, even in very poor parts of the country.

Today our principal concern is no longer with churches built of stone, but with living churches, human creatures, temples of God.

I feel happy when I meet the new-style missionaries here. By the Holy Spirit's light, these priests, nuns and lay-people have grasped that the real task to be done is not building fine churches, big schools, fine hospitals, is not providing solutions, nor even working for the people, but being with the people. And that's exactly where they are. They live with the poor. If the water-point is a long way away and you have to walk all the way home with a jerrycan of water on your head, this is what the priests do too, what the nuns do too.

Today's missionaries know the Lord was here before they arrived. The Spirit of God had sown the seeds of truth beforehand.

I have often experienced this. I read a passage from the Gospel to a mixed group of educated people and poor people who don't know how to read or write. When I invite comments, the most apt, the most vivid, the most penetrating ones come more often than not from the illiterates. Then I understand those words of Christ's: 'I thank you, Father, for hiding these truths from the powerful and the learned and revealing them to mere children.'

Our chief concern today is with helping even those who are in the direst poverty to realize they are children of God, to behave as children of God, having heads to think with and mouths to speak with, in communities.

I set my hope in these little communities, relying on themselves and one another to safeguard human rights, receiving brotherly and sisterly support from other groups in wealthier countries and, assisted by the Spirit of God, determined to create a more just world where we can breathe more freely.

This is indeed the work of the Spirit of God and not of human agency. The Lord wants the whole human race to end up as one family: God's family.

5

Herod was furious on realising he had been fooled by the wise men, and in Bethlehem and its surrounding district he had all the male children killed who were two years old or less, reckoning by the date he had been careful to ask the wise men. (Matt. 2:16)

The Massacre of the Innocents, Dom Helder: don't you get the feeling that this is still going on?

Yes, I do. And this is the form, as I see it, the Massacre of the Innocents takes today.

It's not for me to judge. I don't really know who are directly responsible. But my own feeling is that, rather than have the guts to face up to the radical changes which the politics, for instance, of international trade now require, some wealthy countries find it easier to hand out pills all over the world and in particular to the poor. At the same time they promote the idea that if there's no development in under-developed countries, this is because the poor don't understand the need for birth control.

Instead of a radical rethinking of the relations between industrialised countries and poor countries that produce the raw materials, it is much more convenient to spread the idea that the poor should limit the number of children they have.

But that's all wrong! The cause of under-development isn't the population explosion; it's the explosion of self-centredness. The day we manage to control self-centredness, to revise in depth the structures of injustice, we shall see that God was not mistaken in creation.

There's enough land for everyone, there's enough food for everyone. But as long as we put profit before humanity, we shall always end up in these same idiotic situations: over-production here, under-nourishment there. It's incredible, in the age of the computer and space travel: the human race, as far as brain-power is concerned, shows that it truly shares in God's creative power, yet when it comes to will-power, we're still no better than monkeys. We're unable to overcome our own selfishness.

That's why the Massacre of the Innocents still goes on.

6

Three days later, they found him in the Temple, sitting among the teachers, listening to them, and asking them questions; and all those who heard him were astounded at his intelligence and his replies. They were overcome when they saw him, and his mother said to him, 'My child, why have you done this to us? See how worried your father and I have been, looking for you.' He replied, 'Why were you looking for me? Did you not know that I must be in my Father's house?' But they did not understand what he meant. And he went down with them and came to Nazareth and lived under their authority. His mother stored up all these things in her heart. And Jesus increased in wisdom, in stature, and in favour with God and with people. (Luke 2:46–52)

This is all the Gospels have to tell us about Christ's life until he was thirty. Don't you think this leaves a distressing gap in our knowledge of the historical Jesus?

No. This doesn't worry me in the least. We already have our work cut out to live like the Christ we do know.

I assure you, I often meet Christ among the teachers. There we are, we educated people who have been to school and university; there we are, reading a page from the Scriptures with simple, illiterate people, and very often the profoundest comment comes from someone who is like a child, like the twelve-year-old Christ. . .

Then again, I relive this scene when teachers come to us from Europe, the United States, from Canada. They are teachers because they've learnt from books, they've listened to important professors. They come here, they listen to life, they learn from life. And they too are dumbfounded.

So it is with the Bible, the Word of the Lord. The Lord spoke. We have an ever increasing respect for the Holy Bible. But when we read the words the Lord uttered, what matters most is that what he said then should help us to hear and grasp what he is saying now. For the Lord is still alive, still listening to the clamour of his people. He still speaks. And it is ours to discover what the Lord is saying through contemporary events.

So then: where was Christ and what was he doing between the age of twelve and thirty? As far as I'm concerned, this isn't a problem since I meet Christ at all ages. I met him in the living cribs in the homes of the poor. I meet him at the age of four, of twelve, of eighteen. Why should I worry my head about what Christ was like when he was eighteen, twenty, twenty-five? I see him in all these remarkable young people insisting on an honest approach to life. How demanding they are! And what a good thing it is they are so demanding.

They insist their parents should practise what they preach and they take them to task when they don't.

At high school and at university they refuse to be fed stereotyped platitudes that don't accord with the facts. They expect their teachers to equip them to cope with the pressing problems of our times. Learning about the past is all very well, but only for the light it can shed on the present and future. They don't want museums; they want living universities.

They are also demanding with priests and bishops and the Pope. And a good job too!

If, in the home, in the schools, in the universities, in the Church, we adults have the guts to take the demands of the young seriously, we shall then have the moral authority to say: 'Friends, we accept your criticisms even if they are rather harsh now and then. Thank you for them, all the same. We find them very helpful. They oblige us to re-think, to correct, to make sporadic progress. But precisely because you demand so much of your parents, teachers and pastors, you will have to be just as demanding with yourselves. Yes, demand a lot of yourselves.'

7

Then Jesus appeared: he came from Galilee to the Jordan to be baptised by John. John tried to dissuade him, with the words, 'It is I who need baptism from you, and yet you come to me!' But Jesus replied, 'Leave it like this for the time being; it is fitting that we should, in this way, do all that uprightness demands.' Then John gave in to him. (Matt. 3:13–15)

By this time Jesus was a man. And, following his example, responsible, thoughtful adult members of the early Church presented themselves for baptism. Later, baptism came to be conferred on children, on babies, too young to take decisions for themselves or to bind themselves for the future. Today there is considerable support for the view that baptism should only be conferred on adults. As a bishop, what is your opinion on this?

Parents are prepared to bring children into the world without consulting them. They give them names – the name you're given is something very important. They teach them a language. They take much longer training them for life than animals do with their young, since the human child is so much weaker. . .

So why, having brought them into the world, given them a name, taught them a language and started to train them for life, why shouldn't parents also initiate their children into a life of dedication to the Lord?

After baptism, next we have confirmation. That's when the child, no longer being carried in someone else's arms but on its own two feet and with a mind of its own, can come and say: 'I've thought over what my parents have done and now, before the Lord and my fellow human beings, I am ready to say I honestly wish to be a Christian to the end of my days.'

What is so wonderful here in our country is that even in the big cities there are more and more little communities. In them, baptism and the other sacraments are lived in a community spirit.

Baptism isn't merely an occasion for inviting family, friends and the priest to a little party. It's the first stage of initiation into the Christian life. And this isn't solely the responsibility of parents. Far from it. It's the whole community who have to set an example for this little one now starting out on the Christian pilgrimage. The community has already prepared itself to welcome a new Christian. A community baptism is a fine thing. Even finer is a community confirmation. For then the young Christian is there to make a personal commitment, and the community is there to listen and support. As for a wedding, a first communion or an ordination in a community. . .

> *St Matthew continues his account of what happened on the banks of the Jordan like this: 'As soon as Jesus was baptised he came up from the water, and suddenly the heavens opened and he saw the Spirit of God descending like a dove and coming down on him. And a voice spoke from heaven, "This is my Son, the Beloved; my favour rests on him." ' (Matt. 3:16–17)*
>
> *One can more or less imagine what Jesus was like, particularly if, like you Dom Helder, one has learnt to recognise him in one's neighbour. But it's much harder to visualise the Father, and to visualise the Holy Spirit is almost impossible. . .*

What do you mean? The Holy Spirit is here! Almost tangibly!

To know God the Father, you only have to look at the creation. There are moments when the Creator is almost visible. It's almost impossible to look at the creation without instantly becoming aware that the Creator is here, alive in it.

The Son of God, he too is here, in our neighbour and in ourselves.

As for the Holy Spirit. . . Ah, if you were with the poor, for instance in an evangelistic movement we call 'Brotherly

Encounter', and were to ask who founded the movement, the immediate answer you'd get would be: 'the Holy Spirit'. You might expect them to say it was some bishop or priest. But no: 'It was the Holy Spirit.'

Now I'm going to tell you a true story. There was a woman who had taken on the job of going round her neighbours and encouraging them to stand firm, since they all knew they were threatened with eviction; some great man had bought the land where they were living. She kept saying, 'They can't evict us like this: We're God's creatures, God's children. There's such a thing as human rights, you know!' But at a given moment she found the police at her door and coming into her house. 'Dom Helder, I was trembling,' she told me. For she knew the police don't behave the same way to the poor as they do to the rich. The poor have no resources, no lawyers, to defend them. 'I was trembling,' she went on. 'I was simply panic-stricken especially when the policemen threw me into the van. Then I said, "Lord, you promised us if we were dragged into court, the Holy Spirit would be with us." I was still trembling. I was ice-cold with fear. But when I appeared before the big landlord who was to interrogate me, I felt the warmth coming back. It was the Spirit of God. I gave amazing, devastating answers. I couldn't begin to tell you now what they were, they were so good!'

That's how we know the Holy Spirit is here, present, alive. Never tell me it's hard to visualise the Holy Spirt. The Holy Spirit is our contemporary, living with us, helping us. What could our weakness do in moments of crisis, were it not for the strength of the Spirit of God?

8

Filled with the Holy Spirit, Jesus left the Jordan and was led by the Spirit into the wilds, for forty days being put to the test by the devil. During that time he ate nothing and at the end he was hungry. Then the devil said to him, 'If you are Son of God, tell this stone to turn into a loaf.' But Jesus replied, 'Scripture says: Human beings do not live on bread alone.'

Then leading him to a height, the devil showed him in a moment of time all the kingdoms of the world and said to him, 'I will give you all this power and their splendour, for it has been handed over to me, for me to give it to anyone I choose. Do homage, then, to me, and it shall all be yours.' But Jesus answered him, 'Scripture says: You must do homage to the Lord your God, him alone you must serve.'

Then he led him to Jerusalem and set him on the parapet of the Temple. 'If you are Son of God,' he said to him, 'throw yourself down from here, for scripture says: He has given his angels orders about you, to guard you; and again: They will carry you in their arms in case you trip over a stone.' But Jesus answered him 'Scripture says: Do not put the Lord your God to the test.' Having exhausted every way of putting him to the test, the devil left him, until the opportune moment. (Luke 4:1–13)

Dom Helder, do you believe in the Devil?

If he had the effrontery to tempt Christ himself, you may be sure he is still around to tempt the Church which is the continuation of Christ's life on earth.

The three temptations can be summed up in one: the temptation of prestige, of power. And this is the very temptation forever confronting the Church.

The Church is divine as to its Founder, but is at the mercy of our own human weakness and more particularly that of its pastors, its bishops and even its pope. Very often we don't even realise we're contributing our own weaknesses to the Church, and even when we do we don't succeed in ridding it of them.

One day someone gave the pope an estate. Other estates were later added to this one. And in no time at all you had the Papal States. The pope had become a king. The worst of it is, once you own estates, you've got to defend them. How would you react if you read in today's paper that the pope was calling on Christians to fight in defence of the Vatican? It would be laughable. Nonetheless there have been warrior popes in times past. . .

But even at the mercy of our weakness, the Church still belongs to Christ. The Spirit of God watches over it. So, once the Lord saw that our weakness couldn't rid the Church of the Papal States, as easy as winking he raised up, in the cause of the unification of Italy, a fellow called Cavour and another called Garibaldi. And piff went the Papal States!

Today the Church is in trammels again, this time of money and profit. At every level from diocese to Vatican, not excluding religious congregations, the Church needs money for worship, for the missions, for social aid. For this money not to be whittled away by inflation, it has to be invested. And then you get clergy caught up in the trammels of finance and regarding human labour purely in terms of its economic yield.

Unless I am mistaken, we clergy have a duty to bring about those changes in the Church which we are demanding of society.

When once again the Lord discovers we haven't the guts to do it, the Spirit will find a way of tearing the Church free of our weaknesses. I don't know when, I don't know how. But I do know the Spirit of God will tear the Church of Christ

29

free of the trammels of money. 'Tear' is the word. It will emerge bleeding and naked, more beautiful than ever.

Dom Helder, have you yourself ever experienced or felt the presence of Satan, as the Curé d'Ars did?

To be sure, there are many, many temptations that can make us slip or fall. But what makes me feel very happy is that there are also many, many calls that come from the Spirit of God to support and help us.

Some people, feeling sorry for themselves, say to me, 'How hard, how frightful it is, living today. You can't set foot outside the house without being harassed by one temptation after another. It's appalling!'

I agree. But I know that today as always we live immersed in God. God isn't in front of us or beside us. We're immersed in God. We walk inside God, we talk inside God. What temptation can floor us if we are inside the Lord?

I'm very fond of travelling by plane, forty thousand feet above the sea. It makes me think of huge birds with enormous wings. And of the Spirit of God hovering over the waters. The Greeks dreamed up every kind of beauty. But there are some beauties the Greeks couldn't even have conceived of: seeing the clouds from above the clouds, gazing at the earth from high above. . .

Even so, one day, I thought: Suppose something goes wrong with the engine. In an instant we shall plummet down and be drowned and the sharks will come. . . For a few seconds this made my flesh creep. But I very quickly thought: Don't worry, old friend. If you fall into the sea, to the bottom of the sea, the Lord will be there, present, with you.

Remember:

> If you take the wings of a bird
> If you go to the end of the earth
>   The Lord is there.
> If you rise to the height of heaven
> If you dive to the depths of the sea
>   The Lord is everywhere.

So you see, if there are temptations, by which I mean provocations to selfishness, fear and hatred, the presence of God is very much stronger. We have God on our side.

Some people go through agonies because they see temptation everywhere, sexual temptation especially.

When I was auxiliary bishop to the Archbishop of Rio de Janeiro, Cardinal Camara, a very good and very conservative man, I remember one Sunday we were driving towards Copacabana Beach. The first bikinis had begun appearing. At a certain moment a girl in a bikini crossed the road in front of the car. She had just come out of the sea. I was entranced. The water was streaming from her hair, her face, her hands. I couldn't stop looking at her. But I sensed that my cardinal was perhaps a trifle worried at the way I stared, the way I smiled. So I said, 'Cardinal, now you can see how hard it is to judge. While I was following that girl with my eyes – I tell you this before the Lord – I was thinking: It's like that when we come out from mass. We've been immersed in the Lord, and grace streams from our fingers, from our hands, from our whole body. I love looking at the human body. It's the masterpiece of creation. There are such beautiful faces! But the picture I was seeing was this one . . . of when we come out from mass. . .'

Does it seem strange to you that Jesus should have consented to converse with Satan?

According to Catholic doctrine, Satan is an angel. He has fallen but he's still an angel. He was created by God.

Jesus lived for forty days in the wilds. Following his example, many Christians have dedicated themselves to God by forsaking the world. Have you ever been attracted to the solitary life, to living as a hermit?

Some people can't converse with the Lord in a crowd. I happen to find it quite easy, however large the crowd may be.

But I do, in a manner of speaking, have my own little wilderness. I mean my 'vigils'. There I meet the Lord and the Trinity. But I do understand about withdrawing to pray in the wilds, provided you take all the cares, preoccupations and problems afflicting humanity with you.

I'm very fond of Thomas Merton. In fact I've even been awarded the Thomas Merton Prize. Thomas Merton was a Trappist monk. He lived the solitary life but he peopled his solitude with the problems of the world. In this peopled solitude, one day he discovered the silliness of racism, another day the horror of war and the dead-weight of injustice. Before writing about these problems, he was welcome everywhere, in every diocese and parish. But afterwards he lost his prestige. That was when he experienced true poverty. I'm convinced the greatest compassion today consists in striving to see justice done, and the greatest poverty is in suffering the consequences of striving for justice.

The wilderness I understand is the one that doesn't entail being remote from people. Being with God, yes; but taking others with you. Like mass for instance: we're there as ambassadors. I like to say, 'Lord, I feel myself to be a worthy ambassador of human weakness. For there is no weakness we the shepherds haven't already known or may not know tomorrow. Not one weakness, not a single sin. . . So Lord, I'm well qualified to speak for all my brothers and sisters, sinners of yesterday, today and tomorrow.'

We talk a lot about sins, but I am happier talking about weaknesses. We even talk of mortal sins. But the Church teaches that, for there to be mortal sin, there must be grave matter, full awareness and total consent. This means that even when the offence to God is grave, if consent is not total or if awareness is not full, it isn't a mortal sin.

Whenever you know people from the inside, you realise there's much more weakness than malignity. And I know Christ loves repeating, 'Father, forgive them, they don't know what they're doing.' This is always my trust, my hope, when I hear of someone being written off as monstrous, perverse, beyond redemption.

Malraux said he couldn't visualise God but understood what Satan was like from seeing concentration camps.

32

When you think not only of concentration camps but of torture and the way we're prepared, with our God-given intelligence, to keep more than two-thirds of the human race in sub-human conditions, it's all too obvious that, as well as the presence of God, there's another presence, very strong, which you well may call diabolic.

9

One of these two who became followers of Jesus after hearing what John had said was Andrew, the brother of Simon Peter. The first thing Andrew did was to find his brother and say to him, 'We have found the Messiah' – which means the Christ – and he took Simon to Jesus. Jesus looked at him and said, 'You are Simon son of John; you are to be called Cephas' – which means Rock.

The next day, after Jesus had decided to leave for Galilee, he met Philip and said, 'Follow me.' Philip came from the same town, Bethsaida, as Andrew and Peter. Philip found Nathanael and said to him, 'We have found him of whom Moses in the Law and the prophets wrote, Jesus son of Joseph, from Nazareth.' Nathanael said to him, 'From Nazareth? Can anything good come from that place?' Philip replied, 'Come and see.' (John 1:40–6)

A single look, a single word, and the disciples forsake all to follow Jesus. Have you ever come across similar lightning conversions or vocations? Are they within your own experience?

You know, whenever there's a member of the laity or a priest or a bishop somewhere trying with might and main to live the Gospel and live it joyfully – I don't mean frustrated, gloomy Christians – then, yes, there will be conversions and vocations. People come, introduce themselves, are there; they follow and sometimes even take the lead. The essential thing is to meet someone with reasons for living to be shared.

But why should Simon, Philip and Nathanael be called and not all the other people Jesus met that day?

At first sight this may seem a little unfair. But not really! The Lord doesn't stint himself to anyone. When his choice lights on someone, when he gives more abundant graces to this person rather than to that, he isn't being unfair, since he makes demands corresponding to the measure in which he gives.

When we're called, it isn't because we deserve to be. No one deserves to be called to life, nor to the Christian life, nor to the apostolate. More especially, no one deserves to be called to be a martyr – that eighth beatitude. When the Lord fixes his choice, this isn't to reward merit, nor is it to confer an honour. It's to call that person to serve more strenuously than others, in his name.

This is the way the Lord prefers to act. Naturally he could do things differently and give the same ration of gifts to everyone. If he was nervous, if he was afraid of being criticised (and even then he wouldn't get away with it), he could make up, label and number identical little packets for everyone: same quantity, same quality. The method he's chosen is a different one. He calls Simon: 'You're to be called Peter.' He calls Philip, he calls Andrew. They aren't better than the others. They are answerable for more. They receive more: living for three years, day and night, with Christ. But for this tremendous grace they are answerable to the whole human race forever.

When I think about those first apostles consecrated by Christ, I think about how they too consecrated others, who consecrated others in their turn, and so on down to the present day. So that each apostle of now is linked to an apostle of then. I often wonder which apostle God has linked Dom Helder to. Was it Andrew? Was it Philip? Which one?

But the great apostle is Christ himself. An apostle is an envoy. Christ was the Father's envoy.

And today, as we now know, the envoys, the apostles, aren't only the bishops, aren't only the bishops, priests, monks and nuns. The laity are envoys too.

35

10

On the third day there was a wedding at Cana in Galilee.
The mother of Jesus was there, and Jesus and his disciples
had also been invited. And when the wine ran out, Jesus'
mother said to him, 'They have no wine.' Jesus said,
'Woman, what do you want from me? My hour has not
come yet.' His mother said to the servants, 'Do whatever
he tells you.'

There were six stone water jars standing there, meant
for the ablutions that are customary among the Jews: each
could hold twenty or thirty gallons. Jesus said to the
servants. 'Fill the jars with water,' and they filled them to
the brim. Then he said to them, 'Draw some out now and
take it to the president of the feast.' They did this; the
president tasted the water, and it had turned into wine.
Having no idea where it came from – though the servants
who had drawn the water knew – the president of the feast
called the bridegroom and said 'Everyone serves good wine
first and the worse wine when the guests have had plenty;
but you have kept the best wine till now.'

This was the first of Jesus' signs: it was at Cana in
Galilee. He revealed his glory, and his disciples believed in
him. (John 2:1–11)

What are your reactions to this delightful miracle?

It's great to see Christ attending a party with his disciples
and Mary his mother. So many people with the best of intentions have the idea that Christians and the party-spirit don't
go together.

Anyhow, here's Christ attending a party. The Gospel doesn't say whether there was dancing at it, but I'm sure there was. And Christ didn't want the party to be a failure. He could have turned the wine into water when the party started. But no, he turned the water into wine just as it was finishing. And he did it because our Lady asked him to.

Of course, it isn't a good thing to get drunk, to lose one's senses. But who says drinking a little wine is a sin? I have deepest respect for those Christian communities who abstain from the least drop of wine and alcohol. But in all brotherliness I would remind them that Jesus performed his first miracle by changing water into wine. More important still, when he decided to remain with us through the Sacrament of the Table, he chose bread and wine. Wine, brothers and sisters!

When I was a little boy, we had a woman neighbour who was very good but very strict. One day when I was making a lot of noise, since I behaved like any other normal, healthy child, this neighbour of ours grabbed me by the arm: 'Little boy, stop jumping about like that. The Child Jesus never used to jump about. Stop shouting. The Child Jesus never used to shout. In heaven, children keep quiet and sit still with their arms folded, looking at the Lord.'

Luckily for me, I already knew that this sort of vision of heaven was quite impossible. Heaven – ah me! – is quite different from that.

37

11

When the time of the Jewish Passover was near Jesus went up to Jerusalem, and in the Temple he found people selling cattle and sheep and doves, and the money changers sitting there. Making a whip out of cord, he drove them all out of the Temple, sheep and cattle as well, scattered the money changers' coins, knocked their tables over and said to the dove sellers, 'Take all this out of here and stop using my Father's house as a market.' (John 2:13–16)

Does this incident turn your mind to the way our great pilgrimage centres are invaded by commercial interests purveying articles of devotion?

My first thought is that many extremely well-intentioned Christians seem only to remember this episode, this particular moment in the Gospel, to the exclusion of all the rest. As if Christ were always on the look-out, ready to condemn and drive out. My God! In contrast to this episode of physical force and harsh words directed at the Pharisees, the Gospel contains so many, many more moments of compassion and kindness.

You mention commercialism as invading our great shrines today. These temple merchants, to my way of thinking, are very simple, very naif, very innocent in comparison with the much more serious faults, into which the toils of money drag all too many members of the Church.

These little vendors of candles, medals, statuettes: small weaknesses, yes, no doubt about it, but not the big weaknesses for which we all who comprise the Church are ourselves answerable.

The great weakness, which perhaps might make Christ take up the whip, extends all over the map of the world. On that map you will see a small group of countries becoming wealthier and wealthier by exerting greater and greater pressure on almost the entire human race. This small group of countries is Christian, at least in origin and name: the countries of Europe and North America. And the Christian part of the Third World – Latin America – is now copying the very injustices committed by the wealthy Christian countries. I should think Christ may well consider taking the whip to us from time to time.

12

Now, he came to the Samaritan town called Sychar near the land that Jacob gave to his son Joseph. Jacob's well was there and Jesus, tired by the journey, sat down by the well. It was about the sixth hour. When a Samaritan woman came to draw water, Jesus said to her, 'Give me something to drink.' His disciples had gone into the town to buy food. The Samaritan woman said to him, 'You are a Jew. How is it that you ask me, a Samaritan, for something to drink?' – Jews, of course, do not associate with Samaritans. Jesus replied to her: 'If you only knew what God is offering and who it is that is saying to you, "Give me something to drink," you would have been the one to ask, and he would have given you living water.'

'You have no bucket, sir,' she answered, 'and the well is deep: how do you get this living water? Are you a greater man than our father Jacob, who gave us this well and drank from it himself with his sons and his cattle?' Jesus replied: 'Whoever drinks this water will be thirsty again; but no one who drinks the water that I shall give him will ever be thirsty again: the water that I shall give him will become in him a spring of water, welling up for eternal life.'

'Sir,' said the woman, 'give me some of that water, so that I may never be thirsty or come here again to draw water.' 'Go and call your husband,' said Jesus to her, 'and come back here.' The woman answered, 'I have no husband.' Jesus said to her, 'You are right to say: "I have no husband"; for although you have had five, the one you now have is not your husband. You spoke the truth there.' 'I see you are a prophet, sir,' said the woman. (John 4:5–19)

What are your comments on this passage?

What I find moving is to see Christ, a Jew, not only talking to a Samaritan woman, but also holding a conversation with someone who has already had five men in her life and is now living with the sixth.

I remember half-a-dozen women coming to see me in my house one day. 'Dom Helder,' they said, 'we've no right to be here. We're fallen women. We live in the red-light district. We haven't come to discuss our spiritual problems with you. We've come because we're going to be turned out of the brothel quarter and moved somewhere terribly far away. Even where we are now, we find it terribly hard to make a living. If we have to go further away, we won't be able to make a living at all. Dom Helder, we know you may be willing to stand up for us. You see, we've got no one to stand up for us.'

I was immensely moved by the confidence these unfortunate sisters of ours put in me. We call them 'sinful women'. Sinners! As if we don't all of us have our sins, all of us have our own weaknesses. In our country they are also often known as 'daughters of joy'. But what a hard time they have of it. I was thrilled by the confidence they showed in me, by asking me to stick up for them.

I can easily sympathise with a woman who gives herself in love to a man. But for women to be exploited and manipulated by pimps, to serve the turn of any man who happens to come along and who then treats them in a way he would never dream of treating his wife. . .

So I said, 'Before I give you my answer, I want to show you something written in the Gospel.' And I took the verse where it says, 'The prostitutes will precede you into the Kingdom of Heaven.' What about that!

I was walking along one day to make a sick-call. It was raining very hard. A woman's voice hailed me from a passing car: 'Dom Helder, can I help you? – 'Well, yes, I've got to get to the hospital. Someone's who's sick is expecting me.' – 'OK. I'll get out and the driver can take you there.' – 'No, no, please don't get out. I can get in with you.' – 'I'll go and sit beside the driver and you can have the back to yourself.'

41

– 'Certainly not. . .' But then I realised the woman was a prostitute on her way from the brothel quarter. She didn't want to compromise me.

So I said, 'I absolutely insist! We're all brothers and sisters. I shall sit here in the back, with you beside me.' – 'Oh, Dom Helder, our Lady must have sent you. Yesterday was her feastday. I'm sick. I may die any time. I've been imploring our Lady for a chance to meet you. Look! I've got six handbags. I keep a photo of Dom Helder in each. Now I'm on the point of dying, I think of my past and say, "Lord, I don't deserve anything. But pity me for the sake of my pastor." '

What humility in the woman! And what faith!

When a woman falls into prostitution in our country, it's nearly always due to extreme poverty and hunger, since she has no other means of surviving. But she still retains her faith and her humility. She doesn't deem herself worthy so much as to offer a prayer to Heaven; she would rather cling to her pastor.

I love to see Christ talking like this to a sinful woman, a woman already living with her sixth man. And I love the sight of this sinful woman transformed into an apostle: she went back to Sychar and proclaimed the Messiah. Magnificent!

13

He came to Nazara, where he had been brought up, and went into the synagogue on the Sabbath day as he usually did. He stood up to read, and they handed him the scroll of the prophet Isaiah. Unrolling the scroll he found the place where it is written: The spirit of the Lord is on me, for he has anointed me to bring the good news to the afflicted. He has sent me to proclaim liberty to captives, sight to the blind, to let the oppressed go free, to proclaim a year of favour from the Lord.

He then rolled up the scroll, gave it back to the assistant and sat down. And all eyes in the synagogue were fixed on him. Then he began to speak to them. 'This text is being fulfilled today even while you are listening.' And he won the approval of all, and they were astonished by the gracious words that came from his lips.

They said, 'This is Joseph's son, surely?' But he replied, 'No doubt you will quote me the saying: "Physician, heal yourself," and tell me, "We have heard all that happened in Capernaum, do the same here in your own country." ' And he went on, 'In truth I tell you, no prophet is ever accepted in his own country.' (Luke 4:16–24)

Is it hard, Dom Helder, being a prophet, and being a prophet in one's own country?

I think the word 'prophet' is used in an over-specialised sense, as though the Lord only charged a small number of people with the responsibility of being one. Whereas we all as members of the Church have a prophetic mission. The whole

43

Church is called to be prophetic, that is to say, to proclaim the word of the Lord and also to lend the Lord's voice to those who have no voice, to do exactly what Christ, when reading from Isaiah, declared his own personal mission to be: 'The spirit of the Lord is on me. He has sent me to bring the good news to the poor, to open their eyes and set them free.' This has always been the Church's mission.

As with prophecy, I always say, so with holiness; although admittedly, in the words of the hymn, 'the Lord alone is holy', essentially holy. But by baptism, by sanctifying grace, we are made sharers in the Lord's holiness. This isn't a favour reserved for the few. It's a gift and an obligation for us all. And being holy doesn't mean having visions or working miracles. It means living by sanctifying grace, constantly mindful that we carry Christ within us and that we walk within God.

One day I was taking viaticum to an invalid. This was in Rio de Janeiro. The tram was packed. I kept my feet as best I could. I was carrying Christ. On the tram there was a woman with her children. I looked at them; it was Christ looking at them. There were workmen, a very pretty girl; it was Christ looking at them. Eventually I reached the sick man's house. After hearing his confession, I gave him the host, the eucharistic Christ. And then, for a few seconds, I was tempted to think, 'How dreary the return journey's going to be! I shall be all on my own. . .' But then I thought, 'No, you won't! True, you won't be carrying Christ in the Eucharist any more, but the Lord will still be there, ever present.'

So, being holy isn't an exceptional privilege. How can we get angry if the God of goodness is within us? How can we be jealous if the Lord is with us? How can we be selfish if the God of compassion and sharing is there?

So it is with prophecy. Being a prophet isn't a mission confined to the few. The Spirit of God is on us. Not only on you, or him, or her, or me, but all of us.

14

In the synagogue there was a man possessed by the spirit of an unclean devil, and he shouted at the top of his voice, 'Ha! What do you want with us, Jesus of Nazareth? Have you come to destroy us? I know who you are: the Holy One of God.' But Jesus rebuked it, saying, 'Be quiet! Come out of him!' And the devil, throwing the man into the middle, went out of him without hurting him at all. Astonishment seized them and they were all saying to one another, 'What is it in his words? He gives orders to unclean spirits with authority and power and they come out.' (Luke 4:33–6)

Exorcism has always had its place in the Church's ministry. Have you yourself ever witnessed or taken part in a scene of this sort?

No. I have never seen an exorcism in my life. Nor for that matter a case of 'possession'.

True, when I come across extreme cases of selfishness, I have a feeling that something other than human weakness is at work: the breath, the influence, the strength of a tempter. Similarly when I'm confronted with hatred and torture. It seems so impossible to me that we human beings, or at least we Christians, can't manage to live together as brothers and sisters when we are all children of God.

But I have never attended an exorcism. Before I became a priest, like all other priests I received minor orders. Among the minor orders was that of 'exorcist', conferring power over demons. But immediately next came that of 'acolyte', conferring the power of serving mass. I was excited and delighted by this, since the grace of taking part in the Eucharist is more important than that of casting out demons.

It sometimes happens here that houses are reported to be haunted. But these are always debatable cases. Never in all my time as a bishop have I felt constrained to send an exorcist to sort things out, since it's hardly ever possible to say, 'Only the devil can be responsible for this'. Usually there are other viable explanations.

Also here we have many different types of spiritualism. In some, the spirits are summoned to do good; in others they are summoned to do evil. At crossroads frequently, and particularly on a Friday evening, you will find 'offerings' to the spirits, either to ward off evil or to provoke it.

Once when I was coming home, I found just outside my door an enormous toad with its mouth sewn up. In the symbolism of *macumba*, this was to invoke death on me. But I picked the toad up – not without distaste. I unsewed its mouth and set it free again. On another occasion, there was an extra-special curse – with eggs.

But also in the voodoo communities there are 'mothers of saints' who pray for me. I respect this. I'm convinced the Lord hears everything that comes from the heart.

15

Leaving the synagogue he went to Simon's house. Now Simon's mother-in-law was in the grip of a high fever and they asked him to do something for her. Standing over her he rebuked the fever and it left her. And she immediately got up and began to serve them. (Luke 4:38–9)

So, if the apostle Peter had a mother-in-law, he must have been a married man. Does it seem to you absolutely indispensable these days for a priest to be celibate?

I understand why the Church has chosen this particular discipline. Since one is freer to make a true gift of oneself – and truly to everyone – when one doesn't have a primary obligation to look after one's own wife and children.

If tomorrow I were to find myself once more on the threshold of the priesthood and if then celibacy were voluntary, I don't doubt but that – so as to be able to give myself to everyone – I should still choose not to inhibit my freedom of action by marrying and having a wife and children.

One day some friends came to see me. They were in the habit of meeting as a small Christian discussion group. They had been discussing Dom Helder and what people said about me. They wanted to tell me about their own reservations. We all stayed up until one o'clock in the morning. I listened to their questions and answered them as best I could. Finally, the spokesman of the group said, 'Dom Helder, our doubts are now resolved. But I find myself in a personal dilemma as a result. For if I no longer have any reservations, from now on I ought to behave like you, make a stand like you, be

47

brave like you. But I know for myself that I'm weak and timid and haven't the guts. . .'

To which I replied, 'Friend, consider the difference between us. You're young and I'm an old man. You've got a young wife, you've got two or three children; your wife is actually expecting another one. Whereas I have no one directly dependent on me. So it's much easier for me to be brave. If I were young, a married man and a father, perhaps I too should have to consider more carefully what I might say before saying it. Yes, it's easier for me to be what may seem brave to you. But this is perhaps merely due to my being freer than you are – with the responsibilities that freedom entails.'

This is why I personally love the celibate life.

16

Now, Jesus was in one of the towns when suddenly a man appeared, covered with a skin-disease. Seeing Jesus he fell on his face and implored him saying, 'Sir, if you are willing you can cleanse me.' He stretched out his hand and touched him, saying, 'I am willing. Be cleansed.' At once the skin-disease left him. He ordered him to tell no one, 'But go and show yourself to the priest and make the offering for your cleansing just as Moses prescribed, as evidence for them.' (Luke 5:12–14)

The Gospel records many miracles performed by Jesus. What do you think about them?

I'm no biblical scholar, but when I read the Gospel I can't help feeling these healings have something very important to say to us, responsible as we are for being the living presence of Christ.

One day I was thinking to myself: We ought to have this same power of working miracles; this power of healing could be very valuable today. . .

But in fact the healings do take place. There are always blind people starting to see, deaf people starting to hear, paralysed people starting to walk. There are even dead people coming back to life.

What we have to do is open our eyes and see. See humanity lying wounded on the roads to Jericho. And go near, not pass by like the priest and Levite. And see how the Lord is present there, ever working his cures.

It is wonderful to meet people, who used to look without

seeing or listen without hearing, once their eyes or ears begin to open. It is a wonderful thing when these people stand up and find they can walk.

Oh yes, I'm always coming across miraculous cures.

17

Then fixing his eyes on his disciples he said:

'How blessed are you who are poor: the kingdom of God is yours.

'Blessed are you who are hungry now: you shall have your fill.

'Blessed are you who are weeping now: you shall laugh.

'Blessed are you when people hate you, drive you out, abuse you, denounce your name as criminal, on account of the Son of man. Rejoice when that day comes and dance for joy, look! – your reward will be great in heaven. This was the way their ancestors treated the prophets.' (Luke 6.20–3)

This was the marvellous passage that nearly converted Gandhi and certainly inspired him to action. But other people sometimes see it as an invitation to put up with anything on earth, so as to reap a reward in Heaven. . .

For a start, when Jesus speaks of the blessedness of poverty, he doesn't mean the blessedness of misery. Misery is an insult to the Creator.

Today, what two-thirds of the human race are enduring isn't poverty but misery, hunger. Jesus certainly didn't mean to say that this was blessed.

And take St Francis too: he sang the praises of Lady Poverty, not of Lady Misery. Today he would probably choose Lady Justice.

I think we are perhaps better placed to appreciate the blessedness of poverty when we can see the terrible results produced by insatiable greed for profit and wealth. So many people want more and more than they've got. Not only individuals but countries, continents, empires.

I'm certain that unbridled lust for profit leads to a world gone mad, to suicide.

Each beatitude has a character of its own.

I love it when, through St Matthew, Jesus speaks of the meek who will possess the earth. Not only heaven and eternity, but the earth. I think of this when people deny the efficacy of non-violence: 'If we don't fight back, we shall be crushed!'

I'm not saying being meek, good and kind will get you everything you want. But it's obvious, isn't it, that by meekness, goodness, kindness, you can get what violence can never get. Parents, for instance, are well aware of this, since they know what helps their children to grow up.

Violence can break my body. But inside me there's something that can't be touched. Except by kindness.

Take persecution. Certainly when we love justice, when we fight for justice, we often have to endure being persecuted. In all ages, in all countries, when people are fighting for human rights, they must expect to put up with a certain amount of hardship. But it's a joy to suffer for love of justice. No one has the personal strength or merit to do this, but the Lord comes to our aid; strength wells up inside our weakness.

No, the beatitudes aren't counsels of weakness and they don't lead to weakness.

You know, it's easier to live in hatred than in kindness. Only the strong, strong in the grace of the Lord, can consistently live in kindness. But it's strange to see how the mighty ones of this earth fear kindness. The non-violent represent terrible problems for them. It's very easy to use force against force. But faced with non-violent resistance, the mighty don't know what to do. Their only solution is to kill the leaders of non-violence: Gandhi, Martin Luther King and scores of others whose names don't get into the papers but whom I know – victims of an oppression that non-violence fills with dread.

Oh no, the beatitudes aren't by any means synonymous with weakness.

18

'You have heard how it was said: Eye for eye and tooth for tooth. But I say this to you: offer no resistance to the wicked. On the contrary, if anyone hits you on the right cheek, offer him the other as well; if someone wishes to go to law with you to get your tunic, let him have your cloak as well. And if anyone requires you to go one mile, go two miles with him. Give to anyone who asks you, and if anyone wants to borrow, do not turn away.

'You have heard how it was said, You will love your neighbour and hate your enemy. But I say this to you: Love your enemies and pray for those who persecute you; so that you may be children of your Father in heaven, for he causes his sun to rise on the bad as well as the good, and sends down rain to fall on the upright and the wicked alike. For if you love those who love you, what reward will you get? Do not even the tax collectors do as much? And if you save your greetings for your brothers, are you doing anything exceptional? Do not even the gentiles do as much? You must therefore set no bounds to your love, just as your heavenly Father sets none to his.

'Be careful not to parade your uprightness in public to attract attention; otherwise you will lose all reward from your Father in heaven. So when you give alms, do not have it trumpeted before you; this is what the hypocrites do in the synagogues and in the streets to win human admiration. In truth I tell you, they have had their reward. But when you give alms, your left hand must not know what your right is doing; your almsgiving must be secret, and your Father who sees all that is done in secret will reward you.

'And when you pray, do not imitate the hypocrites: they

love to say their prayers standing up in the synagogues and at the street corners for people to see them. In truth I tell you, they have had their reward. But when you pray, go to your private room, shut yourself in, and so pray to your Father who is in that secret place, and your Father who sees all that is done in secret will reward you.' (Matt. 5:38–6:6)

Do you really succeed in loving your enemies, in praying for those who persecute you or persecute your friends?

This is a question I'm often asked and this is how I reply.

People are always singing my praises. . . It's a frightful thing only to hear praise. Human weakness finds it all too acceptable. Have you noticed how hard it is to be first in the field when praising somebody? You may imagine you're the first, but in fact you're second. Since the first is invariably the interested party himself. Such is human weakness: if you only receive praise and ever more praise, you quite soon start believing you're a very good person, possibly even a saint. Then it's all up with you, since what the Lord loves is humility. Not outward humility but inward humility, humbleness of heart. If you think you can walk on your own, without needing the Lord, the Lord respects your wishes: You want to walk? O.K., walk! And then, over you go and get crushed. . .

So, you know, we ought to be grateful to people who criticise, attack and persecute us. They balance up those who praise us. They remind us we're human creatures with weaknesses of our own.

I love this sermon of the Lord's. It draws our attention to inward quality, quality of heart.

I love hearing that the left hand shouldn't know what the right hand is doing.

I recall a saying of St Vincent de Paul's: 'The right to give has to be won by loving.' It is difficult to give, to give the way Christ taught us. Quite often, when we do some trifling thing, our right hand promptly tells the whole world about it: 'Look what I've done. Look what I've done!' Oh yes, giving is easy enough, I mean giving as a tree gives shade, from our loftiness downwards. But how hard it is to give without humiliating, as a brother only doing his duty, sharing with brothers and sisters what in fact belongs to them too.

Yes, I love this sermon. I feel I'm actually hearing Christ's voice: 'If you want to pray, don't go into the public square for everyone to know how virtuous you are. No, go into your private room. God will listen to your prayer. . .'

Of course, this isn't a prohibition on going to church. Christ himself attended synagogue and temple. But when I'm in church, I ought to behave as though I were in my private room. Not to get myself noticed. And above all not to scrutinise and pass judgement on the other people there, while I'm pretending to pray.

We often have our own ideas about those who come in and those who go out and those who light candles, and under pretext of charity we think, 'But, Lord, how can that woman have the effrontery to come into your house with a reputation like hers? And that mother spending nearly all day here: she'd do better to stay at home looking after her kids.'

So there we are in church, passing judgement, passing judgement. And yet we haven't the right to pass judgement on anybody. Not even the Father passes judgement. He has left all judgement to Christ his Son. And to pass judgement on anybody, you would have to be inside them and perhaps even before they were born. . . Judging is an impossibility.

I can quite see that charity ought to be discreet. But what about justice, which you've just said is the new name for charity? Can you fight for justice without this being seen and known?

Well, of course it's impossible to fight for justice without being seen and even being praised, as well as opposed. But the ideal thing would be, as this sermon of Christ's makes clear, for Christ to be so truly present in us that, when people see what we're trying to do for justice's sake, they would glorify God and not us.

However, friend, we are so very opaque. Most of the time we hide the Lord. We act as a screen between him and other people. The ideal we should strive for is to be transparent, translucent. The day when, looking at us, our brothers and sisters wouldn't see our poor faces, our poor persons, any more, but Christ the Lord. . . ah, how perfect that would be!

19

'In your prayers do not babble as the gentiles do, for they think that by using many words they will make themselves heard. Do not be like them; your Father knows what you need before you ask him. So you should pray like this:

'Our Father in heaven, may your name be held holy, your kingdom come, your will be done, on earth as in heaven. Give us today our daily bread. And forgive us our debts, as we have forgiven those who are in debt to us. And do not put us to the test, but save us from the Evil One.' (Matt. 6:7–13)

I love hearing the apostles ask: 'Lord, teach us how to pray.' We may sometimes think we've learnt how to pray already. All the same, knowing the Lord's Prayer off by heart isn't enough. The important thing is to learn to live the prayer the Lord has taught us.

Beginning with 'Our Father'. Are we really convinced that God is the Father of us all? Not merely 'my' Father, but 'our' Father. If he is 'ours', then we are all brothers and sisters. People with the same father are brothers and sisters.

It's very easy at mass to say, 'Peace be with you,' to the person standing next to you; but after that we each go home and the other person is forgotten. If the other people were really our brothers or sisters and we knew they were ill, in misery, perhaps even dying of hunger, we should do all we possibly could for them and more. . .

When I was in Rio de Janeiro, one day a man came to see me. He came from Fortaleza, the town where I was born and grew up. He hadn't been able to find a job. I tried to help him. I wrote to a friend of mine who owned a big shop: 'Dear friend, see if you can take Antonio on. He's my brother, my blood-brother. He hasn't any work and he's hungry. Can you give my brother, my blood-brother Antonio, a job?'

My friend was on the telephone to me immediately: 'Look, your brother Antonio's just arrived. I've given him a job. But, Dom Helder, how can your brother have possibly fallen into such misery – your own brother?' – 'Is he really with you already?' – 'Yes, he is. And I've also given him some clothes and shoes since he was looking like a tramp. But I suspect you told me he's your brother so that I wouldn't be able to refuse.' – 'Not at all. He is my brother, I tell you.' – 'Brother, brother: I know, all the world's your brother!' – 'Honestly, he is my brother. We've got the same Father.' – 'Didn't you tell me: blood-brother?' – 'We call those blood-brothers who have the same blood of the same father in their veins. So there you are: Christ shed the same blood for you, for me, for Antonio. So we're brothers in the blood of Christ.'

What a long way we are from knowing how to live 'Our Father'!

Then again, when we say, 'Thy will be done'. It's easy enough to accept God's will when it coincides with our own. We know exactly how to ask the Lord for things, but the Lord had better look out and agree with what we want. And on no account should the Lord think or want anything different.

And yet, very often what we ask for isn't what is good for us. We are like little children, as far as the Lord is concerned. A father knows better than to give his child the knife it wants to play with or to let it go down the stairs on its own.

You know the prayer I love to say? 'Lord, may your grace help me to want what you want, to prefer what you prefer. . .' Want what you want. . . Prefer what you prefer. . . For, honestly, what do we know? We ought to do everything as though all depended on us, at the same time putting ourselves into the Lord's hands, knowing that our own strength lies in offering him our weaknesses.

We really need to learn to live Christ's prayer. To learn for instance how to share our bread. When we pray, we know we've got bread at home, not only for today but for the whole month, perhaps for the whole year and even for the rest of our lives. There wouldn't be any problems if, as well as ourselves who have enough bread for the rest of our lives and even for our heirs, there weren't our brothers and sisters who haven't even got their daily bread and who endure hunger in misery.

If only we Christians, charged with the terrible responsibility of bearing the name of Christ, if only we could at least really behave like brothers and sisters.

I remember seeing a Franciscan going by one day, and thinking, 'How rash, how brave, to bear the name of Francis of Assisi.' And we who are brave and rash enough to bear the name of Christ, what about us who call ourselves Christians? What a responsibility we have!

In Rio de Janeiro where I lived for twenty-eight years, there was an Italian sculptor. His mother had stayed behind in Italy. One day she wrote to me and said, 'Dom Helder, would you please go to my son's studio. He isn't well. He ought to see a doctor. I can't persuade him to go.'

I went to see him in his studio. True artist that he was, he couldn't spare a glance for the statues he'd already completed. For artists are dreamers. And when they dream, they feel practically sure that this time they'll manage to translate the dreamed ideal into reality. Having finished the work however, they find the result so disappointing, so pathetic compared with what they imagined, that they instantly start dreaming all over again. Hence this sculptor's attention was exclusively directed to two statues he was in the act of creating. He kept going to and fro from one to the other, enraptured, like God at the dawn of creation.

To carry out my mission, I tried to speak to him about his health and seeing the doctor. Once, twice, three times, four, five. At the sixth, he exploded, 'If you aren't interested in the works I'm creating, get to hell out of here!'

It was then I realised, it's not enough to go into a church and say, 'Lord, Lord. . .' We must look at, admire and love the Lord's masterpiece: the human creature.

Yes, the Lord requires that, having prayed and, precisely because we have prayed, being filled with the Spirit of God, we turn our gaze on our human brothers and sisters.

59

20

When he went into Capernaum a centurion came up and pleaded with him. 'Sir,' he said, 'my servant is lying at home paralysed and in great pain.' Jesus said to him, 'I will come myself and cure him.' The centurion replied, 'Sir, I am not worthy to have you under my roof; just give the word and my servant will be cured. For I am under authority myself and have soldiers under me; and I say to one man: "Go," and he goes; to another; "Come here," and he comes; to my servant: "Do this," and he does it.' When Jesus heard this he was astonished and said to those following him, 'In truth I tell you, in no one in Israel have I found faith as great as this. And I tell you that many will come from east and west and sit down with Abraham and Isaac and Jacob at the feast in the kingdom of Heaven; but the children of the kingdom will be thrown out into the darkness outside, where there will be weeping and grinding of teeth.' And to the centurion Jesus said, 'Go back, then; let this be done for you, as your faith demands.' And the servant was cured at that moment. (Matt. 8:5–13)

Whenever I hear this passage read, I always wonder how there can be people silly enough to believe that only Catholics will be saved. As though the Holy Spirit were up there, singling out the Catholics or possibly the Christians, to breathe on them and only them. . .

No! Wherever in the world there are human creatures hungering and thirsting to love and help, trying to overcome self-centredness, escaping from self, caring for their neighbours, listening to the voice of conscience, striving to do good, the Spirit of God is with them. I love the Lord's words: 'Many will come from the East and from the West. . .' In the Father's house we shall meet Buddhists and Jews, Moslems and Protestants – even a few Catholics too, I dare say.

All too often we believe we have a monopoly of the truth. But the truth is so enormous. God, for instance. We live within God and we have God within us. But God is so great that, for us to comprehend – and comprehend means embrace – God completely, we should have to be even greater than God is.

I was very excited when the first photos were taken of the hitherto unknown, invisible side of the moon.

What a surprise it will be when one day we see the Father face to face. Then we shall realise how poor, limited and imperfect a vision of God we have now.

And the same goes for truth. We have no monopoly of the Holy Spirit. We should be humble about people who, even if they have never heard the name of Jesus Christ, may well be more Christian than we are.

21

Now, one day he got into a boat with his disciples and said to them, 'Let us cross over to the other side of the lake.' So they set out, and as they sailed he fell asleep. When a squall of wind came down on the lake the boat started shipping water and they found themselves in danger. So they went to rouse him saying, 'Master! Master! We are lost!' Then he woke up and rebuked the wind and the rough water; and they subsided and it was calm again. He said to them, 'Where is your faith?' They were awestruck and astounded and said to one another, 'Who can this be, that gives orders even to winds and waves and they obey him?' (Luke 8:22–5)

This is a scene for all times and every day. Naturally we think of the storms tossing the Barque of Peter, the Church. We are frightened by these monstrous waves, the roaring thunder. And Christ sleeps on. . .

Wonderful to see Christ sleeping through the storm. This is to test our faith and make it stronger.

I sometimes like to think we oughtn't to wake the Lord. Let him sleep. He's here. And because he's here, it's impossible for the boat that's carrying him to sink. We passengers can keep calm, even when the hurricane's at its worst.

I'm not above fear. Not at all, I'm as human as anyone else. But what I'm saying is that knowing Christ is here in the same boat ought to help us keep confident and keep smiling.

One day I was on the Sugar Loaf. It's lovely on the top of this mountain. A storm broke out. It was even lovelier, an incomparable sight. Round me, people were trembling at the lightning. I felt it wouldn't be human not to share their fear and instead give the impression that I was tougher and different, and stay there gazing rapturously at the sky. It wasn't bravery but the grace of the Lord that filled me with wonder at this prodigious storm. So I did my best to cheer the others up: 'Don't worry, it will soon be over.' But I couldn't bring myself to say what I was actually thinking: 'Look at how lovely it is!' In fact I was imagining that in a flash the heavens would part and we should all see the Lord up there. It was fantastic!

22

When he reached the territory of the Gadarenes on the other side, two demoniacs came towards him out of the tombs – they were so dangerously violent that nobody could use that path. Suddenly they shouted, 'What do you want with us, Son of God? Have you come here to torture us before the time?'

Now some distance away there was a large herd of pigs feeding, and the devils pleaded with Jesus, 'If you drive us out, send us into the herd of pigs.' And he said to them, 'Go then,' and they came out and made for the pigs; and at that the whole herd charged down the cliff into the lake and perished in the water.

The herdsmen ran off and made for the city, where they told the whole story, including what had happened to the demoniacs. Whereupon the whole city turned out to meet Jesus; and as soon as they saw him they implored him to leave their neighbourhood. (Matt. 8:28–34)

This is a very obscure story. Even so, it comes in the Gospel. . .

There are some obscure passages in the Gospel. I think anyone who claims to understand everything in Holy Scripture, as in life, can't be altogether human.

For my part, I have a number of mysteries stored up in my mind. When I reach the Father's house, I shall have several questions I want to ask the Lord. Not straightaway, since I shall be overjoyed at seeing the Lord face to face and being with my brothers and sisters. But later on, after a few days. Of course, this is only a manner of speaking, since face to face with the Lord all mysteries vanish – a way of saying that in our small corner of planet Earth, this speck in the universe, we can't see or understand everything.

The sufferings of the innocent for instance, above all those of little children. This is a constant problem, a mystery, to me. I say, 'Lord, I don't pretend to understand you. Still less do I presume to judge you.' But the problem doesn't go away. It will of course be resolved the moment I reach the Father's house. But I shall still feel like saying, 'Father, I know you're a real father. But why, Father, do you build life on death?'

Talk about hyenas: we human beings are like hyenas ourselves, only somewhat more sophisticated. To keep ourselves alive, we kill cows, sheep, pigs. We live on the deaths not only of animals but of vegetables too. The whole chain of existence is made up of thousands of deaths.

I am Archbishop of Olinda and Recife. For me to be here, someone had to die before I came – my predecessor. And it's always like this. There's only one example of life not being born from death, and that's the Holy Trinity. The Father who for all eternity begets the Son. The Father and Son who together give life to the Spirit. This is Life, Life and only Life. But apart from the Creator and the angels, there is always the same terrible mystery: life that sustains itself on death.

This is a colossal question which human weakness can never hope to solve. But I can tell you, once I stand before the Lord, I shan't even have to ask it. . .

23

Now while he was at table in the house, a number of tax collectors and sinners came and sat down at table with Jesus and his disciples. When the Pharisees saw this, they said to his disciples, 'Why does your master eat with tax collectors and sinners?' When he heard this he replied, 'It is not the healthy who need the doctor, but the sick. Go and learn the meaning of the words: Mercy is what pleases me, not sacrifice. And indeed I came to call not the upright, but sinners.' (Matt. 9:10–13)

I love this passage. In it I really and truly meet the Lord, the Christ.

Christ shows great understanding, great patience with all sinners, all sins. Except pharisaism. Pharisaism is when we consider ourselves to be better, holier than other people. This the Lord will not put up with.

I have the story of the Pharisee and the tax-collector in mind. The Pharisee was confident of his righteousness. He used to go to the temple so that everyone could see him. And he uttered a very peculiar prayer, which we often utter too. He recited his own praises; then, looking at the tax-collector, he said, 'I say, Lord, how can that fellow have the cheek to come into your house? That miserable wretch, that thief!'

Whenever we pass judgement and condemn someone, this is because deep down we consider ourselves to be different: 'I'm not this. I don't do that. . .' If I were or did what I condemn, I shouldn't condemn. But I think I'm different, more righteous. Yet the tax-collector will go home forgiven and the Pharisee will remain with his pride.

I remember one day during the Council, when I began carrying a cross made of wood, the photographers wanted to take me with my fellow-bishops who were carrying lovely golden ones. I said, 'My friends, if this wooden cross doesn't manage to convey what is going on in my heart, if it only serves to set me apart from the "bourgeois" bishops and proclaim that I am humbler, nearer to the poor than they are: then I'm done for. For without humility and without love one can't take a single step in the way of the Lord.'

24

Jesus made a tour through all the towns and villages, teaching in their synagogues, proclaiming the good news of the kingdom and curing all kinds of disease and all kinds of illness.

And when he saw the crowds he felt sorry for them because they were harassed and dejected, like sheep without a shepherd. Then he said to his disciples, 'The harvest is rich but the labourers are few, so ask the Lord of the harvest to send out labourers to his harvest.' (Matt. 9:35–8)

At a time when the Church is short of vocations, don't you think these words have a very topical ring?

I'm going to tell you how I see the problem of vocations here in Brazil, in Latin America. I'm not talking about other countries in other continents.

We have experienced a very intense form of clericalism here. That is to say, for centuries priests were necessary everywhere for everything. Even when the laity were supposedly called upon to help, decision-making and overall responsibility rested with the clergy. Without priests, no Church.

Today, the Second Vatican Council has helped us to accept, to recognise, to understand the role and mission of the laity. And so, if we really pass all functions not specifically priestly over to the laity and if we see them confidently and joyfully taking on their mission, I can truthfully say that, with far fewer priests, the Church can gather great harvests.

At the same time, where there are priests who are not forever complaining, frustrated and gloomy, but happy in the knowledge that life is the gift of God and that the priesthood is a very fine way of giving oneself to God by giving oneself to others, then, I can truthfully say, vocations abound.

The thing is, today we have to look at the Church as a whole. The Church isn't merely the pope, or the pope and the bishops, or the pope, the bishops and the priests, or even the pope, the bishops, the priests and the members of religious orders. The Church is the laity too. They have a mission to fulfil. An irreplaceable mission of their own, with nothing make-shift or stop-gap about it while priests are in short supply and until there are more of them again. No way!

It isn't easy to learn how to discuss things and how to share responsibility. Especially for us bishops and even those parish priests who can still remember the days of the absolute kings when we were like so many little popes. An honest exchange of views isn't easy. And yet how true it is that meeting someone who doesn't see eye-to-eye with you can be an enriching experience.

Now of course I'm not saying I enjoy being constantly argued with. It's hard for anyone to believe they're never even a little bit right. But even less do I enjoy meeting people who invariably agree one-hundred-per-cent with me. I don't agree one-hundred-per-cent with myself. I argue against myself quite often.

But what a good thing it is to have an honest exchange of views.

25

'Look, I am sending you out like sheep among wolves, so be cunning as snakes and yet innocent as doves.

'Be prepared for people to hand you over to sanhedrins and scourge you in their synagogues. You will be brought before governors and kings for my sake, as evidence to them and to the gentiles. But when you are handed over, do not worry about how to speak or what to say; what you are to say will be given to you when the time comes, because it is not you who will be speaking; the Spirit of your Father will be speaking in you.' (Matt. 10:16–20)

Years ago when I was still at seminary, I used to think this prophecy of the Lord's only applied to the early centuries of Christianity, to the persecutions recorded in church history. But clearly these words are valid for all time. Always, in every corner of the globe, you risk making enemies if you really try to live the Gospel.

Because the Gospel explodes self-centredness. If you make up your mind, with the Lord's grace, to live the Gospel, that is to say, to oppose self-centredness, you will inevitably run into trouble. With yourself and with other people. And not only with governments and powerful individuals, but with churchmen too. And not only with people, but with structures.

I love the passage where Christ says, 'Don't worry. The Spirit of your Father will do the talking.'

It makes me think of one of my priests who was worse than killed, he was butchered, for working for justice with the young. If someone the night before had said, 'Dom Helder, tomorrow one of your priests is going to be sacrificed, murdered; tomorrow you'll have a martyr among your priests,' I should certainly have run through the list of all my priests and tried to guess which of them was to be the chosen one. I could have thought of a dozen, maybe twenty. But I doubt if I should ever have thought of the one the Lord did in fact choose. He was such a modest, candid, simple soul.

Honestly, we don't need to worry about whether we shall have the strength, the courage and the right words to say at the right moment. The strength will not come from us. And the answers will be those of the Spirit of the Father speaking in us.

26

One of the Pharisees invited him to a meal. When he arrived at the Pharisee's house and took his place at table, suddenly a woman came in, who had a bad name in the town. She had heard he was dining with the Pharisee and had brought with her an alabaster jar of ointment. She waited behind him at his feet, weeping, and her tears fell on his feet, and she wiped them away with her hair; then she covered his feet with kisses and anointed them with the ointment.

When the Pharisee who had invited him saw this, he said to himself, 'If this man were a prophet, he would know who this woman is and what sort of person it is who is touching him and what a bad name she has.' Then Jesus took him up and said, 'Simon, I have something to say to you.' He replied, 'Say on, Master.' 'There was once a creditor who had two men in his debt; one owed him five hundred denarii, the other fifty. They were unable to pay, so he let them both off. Which of them will love him more?' Simon answered, 'The one who was let off more, I suppose.' Jesus said, 'You are right.'

Then he turned to the woman and said to Simon, 'You see this woman? I came into your house, and you poured no water over my feet, but she has poured out her tears over my feet and wiped them away with her hair. You gave me no kiss, but she has been covering my feet with kisses ever since I came in. You did not anoint my head with oil, but she has anointed my feet with ointment. For this reason I tell you that her sins, many as they are, have been forgiven her, because she has shown such great love. It is someone who is forgiven little who shows little love.' Then he said to her, 'Your sins are forgiven.' Those who were with him at table began to say to themselves, 'Who is this man, that even forgives sins?' But he said to the woman, 'Your faith has saved you; go in peace.' (Luke 7:36–50)

I like the simplicity with which Jesus accepts the gesture and love of this poor human creature, this sister of ours.

We have so exaggerated the problem of sin. We are such Pharisees. We stick the label 'sinner' on other people as though we had no sins of our own. . . Who can cast the first stone?

Sin. . . Sin isn't what other people say we've done. It's what our conscience tells us: 'You've done wrong. You shouldn't behave like that.'

I well remember a poor woman coming to see me. 'Look, Dom Helder,' she said, 'my story's like many others you've heard already, I'm sure. My mother died. I was brought up by an aunt. One day, when I was with my boyfriend, he made me pregnant. My aunt very brutally threw me out. I ended up with those other women in the brothel quarter.

'Some kind-hearted women happened to notice I was unhappy doing that kind of work, living that kind of life. They told me how I could tear myself away from it and bring up the three kids I had by then. They suggested I rented a little room. They even bought me a sewing-machine.

'You know, Dom Helder, I've done everything I could to satisfy the demands of the grand and beautiful ladies who order clothes from me. But their demands are never-ending. And when it comes to paying, they say, "Come back on the first of the month!" Money's no problem for them. . .

'It's two and a half years now since I tore myself away from the brothel quarter. But since then, on seven or eight occasions, I've found myself without enough money to feed the kids; they've been crying with hunger. So once again I've had to go looking for men.'

She realised that I was upset and trembling. But she went on, 'I don't want to mislead you. I went out looking for men again seven or eight times because my kids were hungry, but three or four times too because the loneliness was so crushing.'

73

Yes, believe me, the Lord understands what victims feel. The Lord isn't here to tot up our unfortunate sisters' sins. They are victims.

We churchmen frequently make too much of women's sins and sexual sins in general. As if sexual sins were graver than sins against compassion. Good heavens! How often we offend against compassion when, for instance, we inveigh against prostitutes.

We must keep the gospel story of the adulterous woman ever in mind. I'm sure it would have been quite easy to find an adulterous man. There's no adulterous woman without an adulterous man. But it was less trouble to seize on the woman, drag her into the square and pass judgement on her. And they were getting ready to stone her to death according to the law. To feel satisfaction, almost joy, at seeing the law enforced even on someone who's actually guilty, may well be a lack of charity.

Ought we to rate sexual sins as worse than sins against compassion?

27

Then some of the scribes and Pharisees spoke up. 'Master,' they said, 'we should like to see a sign from you.' He replied, 'It is an evil and unfaithful generation that asks for a sign! The only sign it will be given is the sign of the prophet Jonah. For as Jonah remained in the belly of the sea-monster for three days and three nights, so will the Son of man be in the heart of the earth for three days and three nights. On Judgement Day the men of Nineveh will appear against this generation and they will be its condemnation, because when Jonah preached they repented; and look, there is something greater than Jonah here. On Judgement Day the Queen of the South will appear against this generation and be its condemnation, because she came from the ends of the earth to hear the wisdom of Solomon; and look, there is something greater than Solomon here.' (Matt. 12:38–42)

By 'the sign of Jonah', wasn't Jesus predicting his own burial?

Predicting his resurrection, rather. How right St Paul was.

On Good Friday, Christ seemed to have failed completely. He had preached as no one had ever preached. He himself had set the example. Crowds gathered wherever he went. His look, his smile, his presence touched their hearts. He performed miracles. And now here he was, being forced to carry a cross and being nailed to that cross, like a failure. For three hours, with no support for his feet, his hands, his head. He was thirsty. He died. He was put to death. He was buried by his mother.

If he hadn't risen from the dead as he foretold, our faith would be meaningless, says St Paul. Our faith would be one huge delusion.

But Christ did rise again. I have no doubt about it. Thousands upon thousands of martyrs have offered their lives to proclaim that Christ did rise again.

So, in those most critical, most agonising of moments, we Christians have no right to forget that we are not born to die; we are born to live.

We must hold on to hope, to inner peace, since we have the deep certainty of having been born for Easter, the everlasting Easter Day.

28

'When an unclean spirit goes out of someone, it wanders through waterless country looking for a place to rest, and cannot find one. Then it says: "I will return to the home I came from." But on arrival, finding it unoccupied, swept and tidied, it then goes off and collects seven other spirits more wicked than itself, and they go in and set up house there, and so that person ends up worse off than before. That is what will happen to this wicked generation.' (Matt. 12:43–5)

We are never completely converted. We have to keep on converting ourselves every day. . .

One day some nuns invited me to say mass to mark the sixtieth year of profession of one of them, a very holy woman. Pretending not to be quite sure what anniversary it was that we were celebrating, I said to her, 'Sister, let me get this straight. Exactly how many years have you spent in the religious life?' Very humbly and first looking round to make sure there was no one else eavesdropping except God, she replied, 'Honestly, Father, I've only spent one day in the religious life. Because every day I have to start all over again.'

What a remarkable answer!

We human creatures bear within ourselves great riches and great weaknesses.

We are living temples, living churches. The Lord is within us, with the Holy Spirit. At catechism, we're taught the seven gifts of the Holy Spirit. Obviously the Holy Spirit isn't so hard-up as to dispose only of seven gifts. We only single out the main ones. But the Holy Spirit has remarkable gifts for each of us. There is no one on whom the Holy Spirit doesn't bestow a tailor-made, personalised minimum of charisms.

But to offset these riches there is always self-centredness too. So we also single out the seven principal manifestations of self-centredness, the 'capital sins': envy, laziness, pride, impurity, avarice. . . But there are many more of them than that. They are called 'capital' because each one of them gives rise to many other weaknesses.

God works this marvel: that even though he resides with us and in us, we still retain our weaknesses. It's up to us to avoid giving way to pride, to keep on the alert. We have to keep the process of conversion going all the time.

At the end of the Council, I was sitting next to the President of the Lutheran World Federation. He said, 'Well, Dom Helder, we've had to wait hundreds of years before getting almost what Luther was wanting. What a wonderful thing it is to see the Roman Catholic Church undertaking its own reformation!' Then, very humbly, he added, 'Perhaps we of the Reformed Church are too proud of being reformed, when what we really need is a new reformation.' To which I replied, 'All of us, friend, and all our churches too, constantly need reforming. Conversion ought to be going on every day, since self-centredness is ever-living. They say it only dies a few hours after we ourselves are dead.'

29

He was still speaking to the crowds when suddenly his
mother and his brothers appeared outside wanting to have
a word with him. But to the man who told him this, Jesus
replied, 'Who is my mother? Who are my brothers?' And
stretching out his hand towards his disciples he said, 'Here
are my mother and my brothers. Anyone who does the will
of my Father in heaven is my brother and sister and
mother.' (Matt. 12:46–50)

I think some people might construe this saying of Christ's as
a piece of demagogy. Here he is, surrounded by the crowd.
Someone informs him that his mother and brothers are
present. He then points to his immediate companions: These
are my mother and my brothers. His disciples must have felt
flattered, delighted. Today the crowd would have raised a
cheer. . .

But the demagogue isn't the one who understands crowd
psychology, nor the one who uses it to get a message across,
but the one who exploits it for private ends, for personal self-
promotion.

The Lord that day was not promoting himself. He was
proclaiming a great truth.

There are also people who consider Christ treated his
mother, Mary, rather shabbily. Yet it was in fact the highest
compliment he could pay her, and he paid it for all the crowd
to hear.

It was like saying, 'Look here, Mary isn't my mother merely
because of something mysterious that happened in her womb.
She's my mother because she listens to my Father's Word.

She listens as no other creature listens to him. She looks after him, she gives his life. This, first and foremost, is why she is my mother.'

Mary lived all the great mysteries of God. What a part she played in the incarnation! What a part she played in the redemption! What a part she plays today in the Church! Believe me, we can feel Mary's presence, she is present in every moment of crisis; as a mother, she is always with us, watching over us.

30

'A sower went out to sow his seed. Now as he sowed, some fell on the edge of the path and was trampled on; and the birds of the air ate it up. Some seed fell on rock, and when it came up it withered away, having no moisture. Some seed fell in the middle of thorns and the thorns grew with it and choked it. And some seed fell into good soil and grew and produced its crop a hundredfold.' Saying this he cried, 'Anyone who has ears for listening should listen!' (Luke 8:5–8)

A first too-hasty reading may leave the impression that the man sowing the seed was a fool. How silly to sow without first preparing the soil! Sowing on the edge of the path? He must have known the seed would be crushed underfoot. Sowing it on rocks? In brambles? Unbelievable! Still he did manage to sow a bit on good soil. . . Some sower!

But I can tell you this: we should all be in trouble if the Lord – for he is the sower – were only to sow the seed on soils already well prepared. Luckily he sows with prodigal liberality. He scatters the seed here and there, this way and that, in the hope that, even on the rocks, some of the seed will sprout. I love this liberality of the Lord.

Even so, I know that I, as a human creature, ought to try to prepare the soil for the Lord's word. But, like him, I also love sowing seed in soils that are not that well prepared. For, if I haven't been able or haven't known how to prepare the soil, the Lord can do in a flash what we ourselves couldn't do in years and years of trying.

From time to time, people say to me, 'You know, Dom

Helder, my father died recently. Yes, he died without having time to think about God. Things had already gone too far . . . I called a priest but it was too late. He couldn't take it in.' As if, to enlighten us from within, the Lord had need of our ears, our eyes, our senses!

I'm certain that at the decisive moments of our lives, the Spirit of God provokes prodigious flashes of light within us. A veritable battle of love breaks out. . .

I know there are tough passages in the Gospel. I listen respectfully when the Lord speaks of the narrow gate. But I can never manage to understand why, in a universe created by the Father, saved by his Son who is also Love, and dwelt in by the Spirit of the Father and the Son, only a handful of people will be received into the joy of Heaven. It doesn't make sense. It certainly isn't the view the Church has adopted. If I were the devil I should be laughing and jeering through all eternity, 'So this is your universe created by love! So this is what your redemption amounts to!' No.

Death will not have the last word. I feel, I know, that the mercy of the Lord will have the last word.

One day I was sitting with a man who had only a few minutes to live. He was agitated: 'Father, Father, I can never be forgiven. I've committed enormous sins, Dom Helder, and the Lord will never forgive me.' – 'Look,' I said, 'I don't dispute the size and enormity of your sins. I grant your sins may be enormous. But I can assure you, the Father's mercy is more enormous still. Large enough to cover all your sins, however enormous they may be. The goodness and mercy of God exceed anything you can imagine.'

31

He put another parable before them. 'The kingdom of Heaven,' he said, 'may be compared to a man who sowed good seed in his field. While everybody was asleep his enemy came, sowed darnel all among the wheat, and made off. When the new wheat sprouted and ripened, then the darnel appeared as well. The owner's labourers went to him and said: "Sir, was it not good seed that you sowed in your field? If so, where does the darnel come from?" He said to them: "Some enemy has done this." And the labourers said, "Do you want us to go and weed it out?" But he said: "No, because when you weed out the darnel you might pull up the wheat with it. Let them both grow till the harvest; and at harvest time I shall say to the reapers. First collect the darnel and tie it in bundles to be burnt, then gather the wheat into my barn." ' (Matt. 13:24–30)

We all prefer the parables we understand best. Of course I accept the Lord's message in its entirety, but I'm free to store up the questions I intend to ask when I reach the Father's house. . . I feel very pleased when the landowner tells his servants, 'Don't be hasty. Let the darnel grow with the wheat.' My question arises when he adds, 'When the time comes, the wheat will be stored in the barn and the rest will be thrown on the fire.'

I know, the Lord is just. But I am particularly fond of those words in the liturgy, taken from Holy Scripture: 'Lord, you are just, and this is why you will show me your mercy!'

Justice means giving to each according to his or her deserts. But we are weakness itself. The Lord knows us better than we know ourselves. Knowing us as he does, it comes as no surprise to the Lord that the weak are weak, that clay is clay. He knows this perfectly well. He made us. He follows us every second. He knows. He knows that in this human world there is far more weakness than wickedness. Weakness is nearly always at the root of it. And by the root is how the Lord always sees us. . .

32

He put another parable before them. 'The kingdom of Heaven,' he said, 'is like a mustard seed which a man took and sowed in his field. It is the smallest of all the seeds, but when it has grown it is the biggest of shrubs and becomes a tree, so that the birds of the air can come and shelter in its branches.' (Matt. 13:31–2)

What Christ is saying here is something you can see and experience for yourself. There is no proportional relationship between individual human effort and result, where proclaiming the Gospel is concerned. And luckily . . . luckily the Lord doesn't insist on success. The Lord does insist on our working, on our collaborating, but doesn't insist on our succeeding. Success is no concern of ours.

I often think of this when I meet people who, having reached the ends of their lives, feel they've achieved next to nothing.

Do you remember that fine film *Monsieur Vincent* about St Vincent de Paul? At one point in it, Queen Anne of France says, 'Oh, Monsieur Vincent! When I see your hands so full and mine so empty, I could die with shame.' Vincent de Paul himself, however, didn't feel his hands were as full as all that. There's a huge disproportion between the way we actually live and the way we dream about living with Christ.

I love the way, when speaking about perfection, Christ is almost – though kindly – making fun of us: 'Be perfect as my Father is perfect.' He says, 'As my Father is perfect.' This is a way of hinting to us that we shall never be as perfect as we dream of being, when we dream with Christ . . . and that, with God's help, we may achieve more than we suppose.

33

As he stepped ashore he saw a large crowd; and he took
pity on them because they were like sheep without a
shepherd, and he set himself to teach them at some length.
By now it was getting very late, and his disciples came up
to him and said, 'This is a lonely place and it is getting
very late, so send them away, and they can go to the farms
and villages round about, to buy themselves something to
eat.' He replied, 'Give them something to eat yourselves.'
They answered, 'Are we to go and spend two hundred
denarii on bread for them to eat?' He asked, 'How many
loaves do you have? Go and see.' And when they had found
out they said, 'Five, and two fish.' Then he ordered them
to get all the people to sit down in groups on the green
grass, and they sat down on the ground in squares of
hundreds and fifties. Then he took the five loaves and the
two fish, raised his eyes to heaven and said the blessing;
then he broke the loaves and began handing them to his
disciples to distribute among the people. He also shared
out the two fish among them all. They all ate as much as
they wanted. They collected twelve basketfuls of scraps of
bread and pieces of fish. Those who had eaten the loaves
numbered five thousand men. (Mark 6:34–44)

I find it very moving to see the Lord so sensitive to people's
needs. He has eyes to see they are hungry. He has ears to
hear the clamour of his people.

As his followers, we have no right to say: 'Our job's to
proclaim the Word, but it isn't our business to worry over
food. Our food is the Bread of Heaven.'

No. We're not shepherds merely of souls. We're shepherds of human beings, souls and bodies – with everything this involves. And today I am more than ever convinced the Lord is demanding of us that we go even further.

If there are people who are hungry, we should busy ourselves about hunger. It isn't the moment for discussing neat theories, for discussing, for instance, whether this is or isn't paternalism. We ought straightaway to start doing whatever is possible, and a bit of the impossible besides. Particularly these days, when we are aware of the scandal of having two-thirds of the human race suffering from hunger and foundering in misery.

And since this hunger, this misery, stems from injustices and unjust structures, the Lord demands of us that we denounce the injustices. This is part of proclaiming the Word. Denunciation of injustice is an absolutely essential chapter in the proclamation of the Gospel. And not merely a duty for the few. It is a human duty for everyone, a Christian duty for all Christians, and an absolute duty for the shepherds.

When some people read the accounts of the multiplying of the loaves, they imagine the Lord only intended to pre-figure the Eucharist. So they go to Holy Communion.

But, Lord, it seems clear enough to me that the very Eucharist itself ought to open our eyes to the misery and hunger of our fellow-beings.

Take the splendid history of the International Eucharistic Congresses. Originally, the primary purpose was to glorify the Lord hidden in the Eucharist. More recently, we have come to realise that Christ, 'the bread of life', 'the shared loaf', is insisting we should turn our attention to the multitudes hungering for friendship, love, understanding, justice, peace, bread.

So we must open our eyes. We must find a way not only of distributing the bread but of multiplying it.

Today Christ tells us it isn't enough to distribute bread to those who haven't got any. The essential thing is to work towards the creation of a more just world, in which there will no longer be a minority owning too much, among such multitudes of hungry people.

34

Jesus left that place and withdrew to the region of Tyre and Sidon. And suddenly out came a Canaanite woman from that district and started shouting, 'Lord, Son of David, take pity on me. My daughter is tormented by a devil.' But he said not a word in answer to her. And his disciples went and pleaded with him, saying. 'Give her what she wants, because she keeps shouting after us.' He said in reply, 'I was sent only to the lost sheep of the House of Israel.' But the woman had come up and was bowing low before him. 'Lord,' she said, 'help me.' He replied, 'It is not fair to take the children's food and throw it to little dogs.' She retorted, 'Ah yes, Lord; but even little dogs eat the scraps that fall from their masters' table.' Then Jesus answered her, 'Woman, you have great faith. Let your desire be granted.' And from that moment her daughter was well again. (Matt. 15:21–8)

This Canaanite woman's humility is an example to us all. But then, you see, the Lord was testing her faith. He was provoking her. And I have the feeling he very often does the same with us.

Sometimes I say this prayer: 'Lord, I feel very much at ease with you, since you're a real friend, a real brother. I know the Father is our real Father. But, Lord, it happens from time to time that our Father gives the impression of being slightly less than a father: there are so many people suffering, calling, pleading. . .'

On behalf of all these, I almost argue with the Father: 'I know you want to test our faith. I know you. But you know our weakness even better. Don't give this impression of being distant, remote, of not listening. I know you're here, quite close, attentive, listening to everything. So why give the wrong impression?'

35

'I am the living bread which has come down from heaven.
Anyone who eats this bread will live for ever; and the bread
that I shall give is my flesh, for the life of the world.'

Then the Jews started arguing among themselves, 'How
can this man give us his flesh to eat?' Jesus replied to them:
'In all truth I tell you, if you do not eat the flesh of the
Son of man and drink his blood, you have no life in you.
Anyone who does eat my flesh and drink my blood has
eternal life, and I shall raise that person up on the last day.
For my flesh is real food and my blood is real drink.
Whoever eats my flesh and drinks my blood lives in me
and I live in that person.' (John 6:51–6)

It is wonderful to have faith. My way of thanking the Lord
for it is to say: Faith isn't any virtue of mine, it's the grace
of Christ.

It is wonderful, when distributing the Eucharist, to be
absolutely certain I'm handing out not pieces of bread but
the living Christ. This gives me immense joy.

And how self-effacing Christ is, how he hides, how he
disappears! I have to protect him. When it's windy for
instance, I have to protect Christ present in the ciborium or
on the paten. Protect him from the wind with my hand. Then
I smile and say, 'Lord, it's amazing. You are the Strong One,
I am human weakness, yet you make yourself so weak, I have
to protect you.'

It's just the same when I meet the poor: I am absolutely
certain Christ is present under the weakness of the poor.

Very frequently, after failing to find work for days on end, the poor end up by taking refuge in drunkenness, to forget, to escape from reality for a bit. And if you want to go on being with them then, you will hear people say, 'But you can't possibly recognise Christ in these idlers, these drunkards. Anyone who wants to work can find work. If they haven't got work it's because they don't want to work. That can't possibly be Christ.'

True enough, when drowned in alcoholic oblivion, the poor do become like things, objects, animals. They lose their self-respect. But when I look at them from close up, I recognise the face of Christ in them.

It can't have been easy on Calvary either, to recognise Jesus in that agonised face covered in spittle, blood, sweat and dust. The prophet said, 'He looks like a worm squashed underfoot.' A worm. Yet it was Christ all the same.

There is the Eucharist of the Blessed Sacrament: Christ's living presence under the appearance of bread and wine. And there is that other Eucharist: the Eucharist of the Poor, under the appearance of misery. The Real Presence in the poor.

I know theologians will raise distinctions: this isn't quite the same thing, there are differences . . . I also know the Lord will judge us by how we have succeeded in recognising and serving him in the poor. He will say, 'I was there, I was that poor wretch. That poor wretch was me!'

We shall be in for some big surprises. Oh yes, we shall get a shock or two.

In a certain sense perhaps we have laid too much emphasis on Christ's uniquely eucharistic presence. He has other ways of being present too. He said, for instance, that where two or three are gathered together in his name, he is there.

I remember one day when a good nun came a long way on foot to take me to her hospital. 'Father,' she said, 'I've come all this way because we've been without a chaplain for a week now and I haven't had the joy of receiving Christ. I need to receive Christ. Give me communion, Father. And if you can manage it, give us a priest too.'

So first I gave her communion. Then I reminded her, 'Mother, dear sister, you spend your days with the living Christ. You are there, with the sick: these are Christ. You tend, you handle Christ with your own hands. This is another

Eucharist, another living presence of Christ, completing his presence in the Eucharist.'

36

When Jesus came to the region of Caesarea Philippi he put this question to his disciples, 'Who do people say the Son of man is?' And they said, 'Some say John the Baptist, some Elijah, and others Jeremiah or one of the prophets.' 'But you,' he said, 'who do you say I am?' Then Simon Peter spoke up and said, 'You are the Christ, the Son of the living God.' Jesus replied, 'Simon son of Jonah, you are a blessed man! Because it was no human agency that revealed this to you but my Father in heaven. So I now say to you: You are Peter and on this rock I shall build my community. And the gates of the underworld can never overpower it. I shall give you the keys of the kingdom of Heaven: whatever you bind on earth will be bound in heaven; whatever you loose on earth will be loosed in heaven.' Then he gave the disciples strict orders not to say to anyone that he was the Christ. (Matt. 16:13–20)

Can we honestly maintain that the mission entrusted to Peter has been worthily discharged through the – shall we say – tumultuous history of the papacy?

If you read the Gospel a little further on, you will meet the same Peter again with the same Jesus. But when the Lord foretells his passion, Peter is not so happily inspired: 'Come on, Lord! What a silly idea! What you're saying is quite unimaginable.' Then Jesus, having previously congratulated him on his remarkable grasp of the things of God, comes out with these terrible words: 'Get away, Satan. You understand nothing about the things of God.'

It doesn't shock me to encounter human weakness in the papacy: the first pope was himself all too human. Remarkable for some of his responses, impressive in his dreams about loving Christ – 'even if all the others desert you'. . . But weak. In the Garden of Gethsemane he slept. When the soldiers arrived he drew his sword. When the servants asked him if he was with Jesus, he didn't want to know him any more.

How well I understand Peter. He's our brother and no mistake. The popes are Peter's brothers. Obviously they have a special charism, but they're human creatures prone to weakness nonetheless.

Pope Alexander VI Borgia was weak, weak, weak in his personal life. But when the moment came for acting as the successor of Peter, he safeguarded what was essential. The Holy Spirit was there.

I like this chap Peter. He's very much one of us. I shouldn't have liked all the popes always to be holy and perfect. Once we human creatures become convinced we cannot fall, we soon find we can't understand other people's weaknesses any more. By allowing us to fall, into the mud if need be, the Lord preserves us in humility. In one of the psalms it says, 'You are good because you have humbled us.'

The Lord made Peter, so weak and so humble, the chief of the apostles. But in the course of history, the Church of the Apostles split apart. And we have come a long way now in our divisions. I remember how at seminary people used to speak of Luther and the other reformers. Today, I'm glad to see, we are having to re-evaluate the figure of Luther. He was a prophet, in his way. He denounced the scandalous abuses at Rome and in the Church. During the Council and on the three occasions when I met John XXIII, I thought, 'If only Luther, still remaining Luther but capable of reasonable discussion as well, had found himself with a John XXIII, we might perhaps have avoided the scandal of schism.'

Efforts are being made everywhere now to reconcile our differences. When I was a boy, priests were still burning protestant Bibles. Today we have the same books, the same texts and, very often, especially when times are bad, we pray and work together. But the divisions have lasted so long and gone so deep that our peoples don't always understand each other even now.

For me, you know, the pope is truly Peter. He's been chosen by the Lord to be, in a very special way, the sign of unity. The pope works for ecumenism.

37

The scribes and Pharisees brought a woman along who had been caught committing adultery; and making her stand there in the middle they said to Jesus, 'Master, this woman was caught in the very act of committing adultery, and in the Law Moses has ordered us to stone women of this kind. What have you got to say?' They asked him this as a test, looking for an accusation to use against him. But Jesus bent down and started writing on the ground with his finger. As they persisted with their question, he straightened up and said, 'Let the one among you who is guiltless be the first to throw a stone at her.' Then he bent down and continued writing on the ground. When they heard this they went away one by one, beginning with the eldest, until the last one had gone and Jesus was left alone with the woman, who remained in the middle. Jesus again straightened up and said, 'Women, where are they? Has no one condemned you?' 'No one, sir,' she replied. 'Neither do I condemn you,' said Jesus. 'Go away, and from this moment sin no more.' (John 8:3–11)

I wish I could have been present to see this. Especially when Christ was calmly writing on the ground. The bystanders must have been intrigued, possibly nervous: What was Jesus writing?

However, despite the warning Christ gave us then, we still go on carrying stones about with us. We always have stones ready for throwing at other people. It's a terrible thing, this mania of ours for passing judgement, judging and condemning. The process of conversion isn't easy. . .

And yet, reaching the state of not judging others any more would be a notable way of avoiding being judged ourselves. For Christ has said, 'Do not judge. You will be judged by the standard by which you have judged!'

If I don't judge, I shall have the magnificent surprise when I reach the Lord's presence and nervously wonder, 'My God, what's going to happen to me now?' of hearing Christ say to me, 'Don't worry, son. You've done your best not to judge. No judgement for you.' Ah, that will be great!

It's difficult not to judge, not to condemn, not to put other people to death, those whom we think evil or dangerous.

I'm thinking, for instance, of the battles that have to be fought against injustices and for more justice. The ideal thing would be not trying to defeat but to convince.

If I had been born into a rich family, a very rich one or even too rich a one, if I had never breathed any other atmosphere, if I had always travelled by car, never venturing into those districts where misery reigns, never hearing, never seeing, I'm sure my own reactions when people spoke to me about injustice would be the same as those I encounter among the rich, the very rich and particularly the too rich.

There are countries which still retain the death penalty. And it happens from time to time that someone is executed who turns out later to have been innocent. Mistakes will happen.

The same with prison: the time will come, I believe, when we shall be ashamed of having thought it quite normal to shut up our brothers and sisters in cages, like hyenas and wild beasts.

Of course society has to be protected against the wrongs a handful of people may commit against the common good. But it's increasingly possible now, given our advances in knowledge, to have recourse to psychology and education in preference to the barbarity of imprisonment and the death penalty.

38

To the Jews who believed in him Jesus said, 'If you make my word your home you will indeed be my disciples; you will come to know the truth, and the truth will set you free.'

They answered, 'We are descended from Abraham and we have never been the slaves of anyone; what do you mean: "You will be set free?" ' Jesus replied, 'In all truth I tell you, everyone who commits sin is a slave. Now a slave has no permanent standing in the household, but a son belongs to it for ever. So if the Son sets you free, you will indeed be free.' (John 8:31–6)

It is rare to meet people who are really free. If we knew how to look, we should see that some people are tied by their hands, others by their feet and others again by their neck. How various are prisons!

It is rare to meet people who can do without masks. Society is so hypocritical, so pharisaic, that even those thirsting to be genuine can rarely be themselves.

It is rare to meet people who aren't afraid. Home is where it begins. Very often the husband hasn't the guts to be as honest as he should be with his wife. And wife with husband. And children with parents.

I remember a girl who went home one day at 10 o'clock in the evening. She explained quite straightforwardly that she'd been out with a boy, a friend, who might soon be her fiancé. She got a very rude reception. The house became very stormy: such thundering, such lightning!

When I happened to be alone again with her parents, I

said, 'If your daughter doesn't tell you the truth next time, you'll have only yourselves to blame. You couldn't put up with the truth.'

How many people do we know who are able to accept the truth, the whole truth?

That's why there's so much cautiousness, so much fear pervading human relationships. And why so few people succeed in being truly free.

The freer you want to be, the closer you must be united to Christ.

39

'I am the gate. Anyone who enters through me will be safe: such a one will go in and out and will find pasture. The thief comes only to steal and kill and destroy. I have come so that they may have life and have it to the full.

'I am the good shepherd: the good shepherd lays down his life for his sheep. The hired man, since he is not the shepherd and the sheep do not belong to him, abandons the sheep as soon as he sees a wolf coming, and runs away, and then the wolf attacks and scatters the sheep; he runs away because he is only a hired man and has no concern for the sheep. I am the good shepherd. I know my own and my own know me, just as the Father knows me and I know the Father; and I lay down my life for my sheep.

'And there are other sheep I have that are not of this fold, and I must lead these too. They too will listen to my voice, and there will be only one flock, one shepherd.' (John 10:9–16)

Jesus says he is the gate, the gate of the sheepfold, of the corral. So why are we often tempted to be the gate ourselves? Besides the true gate – which is Christ – we also set ourselves up as a gate. Everyone's got to go through our gate, ours: our ideologies, our definitions, our ways of doing things. This won't do! Christ is enough. One gate is enough – the Christ.

Christ also tells us he has other sheep. Elsewhere he relates how he leaves the ninety-nine which are well-behaved, to go in search of the hundredth one, which has followed its own devices or perhaps a different shepherd.

Quite often I meet the ninety-nine sheep, frustrated and

even furious because they think the shepherd has deserted them. Why should he bother about the hundredth one? It only had to be well-behaved and sensible like them.

We're like the prodigal son's elder brother. There's nothing at all uncommon about the jealousy displayed by those who have stayed faithful, who have never given offence, who have never grieved their parents. Here we are, faithful, loyal, where we belong, but full of pride. What? Our father is preparing a feast, a banquet for the good-for-nothing who's wasted the family fortune? How unfair! It is a terrible temptation to shut the shepherd up inside our sheepfold, behind our own gate. . .

40

'And who *is* my neighbour?' In answer Jesus said, 'A man was once on his way down from Jerusalem to Jericho and fell into the hands of bandits; they stripped him, beat him and then made off, leaving him half dead. Now a priest happened to be travelling down the same road, but when he saw the man, he passed by on the other side. In the same way a Levite who came to the place saw him, and passed by on the other side. But a Samaritan traveller who came on him was moved with compassion when he saw him. He went up to him and bandaged his wounds, pouring oil and wine on them. He then lifted him onto his own mount and took him to an inn and looked after him. Next day, he took out two denarii and handed them to the innkeeper and said, "Look after him, and on my way back I will make good any extra expense you have." Which of these three, do you think, proved himself a neighbour to the man who fell into the bandit's hands?' He replied, 'The one who showed pity towards him.' Jesus said to him, 'Go, and do the same yourself.' (Luke 10:29–37)

When we priests and bishops have to preach on the parable of the Good Samaritan, we feel embarrassed by Christ's bold portrayal of the priest who takes a look and then goes on his way. We hastily say: 'But of course this was a priest of long ago, under the Old Law.' As if we priests of today had more time and eyes for the poor. Ah, Lord, how well you know us! We are in more of a hurry every day. We have more and more extremely important problems all the time. It's impossible to be concerned with everybody. And how can we tell whether this particular pauper isn't a fraud exploiting people's good-heartedness?

It's very easy to pass by on the other side, even without meaning to, where poverty and misery are concerned.

And yet, in a big city like mine, it's quite easy to come across not only children and women but men too, foraging in dustbins for something to eat. But you have to go about a bit on foot. For if you are always driving in fast cars, too fast, you don't have time to make contact with misery.

One day I was invited to the opening of a big commercial enterprise. The day was very hot. But the director's office was air-conditioned. And the waiters were going their rounds with glasses of whisky. Once round, twice round, thrice round. I chose to drink Coca-Cola: not out of virtuousness, for I very much enjoy a drop of wine and this presents me with no moral problem, but wine doesn't like me. . .

At a given moment, one of the guests came up to me: 'So, Dom Helder, how's your rabble-rousing going? How can you go on having the cheek to say there's misery and hunger in Recife?' Others, emboldened, came up to ask me the same question. So I said, 'Look here, I've been minding my own business but now you've come along and provoked me. Here's my answer. You've all got your cars here, we can go in them, and I'll soon plunge you up to your necks in misery and hunger.'

They accepted the challenge. Within ten minutes, we arrived at one of the municipal dumps where the city's rubbish gets burnt. Before being burnt, the rubbish is tipped out in heaps on the ground. I know the place well. I called a friend of mine over. He is know as 'Doctor Rot'. He's a council employee. But he's also an expert in telling whether thrown-away food is still fit to eat. He adjudicates between first-class food reserved for council employees, second-class food suitable for the people trying to survive thereabout and the crows picking it over like chicken, and third-class food which is salted for all its worth and then sold in fourth and fifth-class cook-shops where anything, to go with alcohol, is better than nothing.

Dr Rot explained all this to the several dozen company directors who had come down with me. I thought they would

104

be appalled. But next day one of them telephoned me: 'Dom Helder, I've had a brainwave. We can do business, make some money, with Dr Rot.' How nauseating!

We are so far from sharing the spirit of the Good Samaritan.

But I'm sure the Samaritan would be doing more today than looking after bandits' victims and having them ride, not on his donkey now, but in his car. He would be dealing with the ever-growing number of victims of injustice. He would be here – he is here – peaceably but boldly fighting against the unjust structures crushing the human race. For it isn't enough to help the victims of evil. Unacceptable evil must be attacked at the roots.

41

In the course of their journey he came to a village, and a woman named Martha welcomed him into her house. She had a sister called Mary, who sat down at the Lord's feet and listened to him speaking. Now Martha, who was distracted with all the serving, came to him and said, 'Lord, do you not care that my sister is leaving me to do the serving all by myself? Please tell her to help me.' But the Lord answered, 'Martha, Martha,' he said, 'you worry and fret about so many things, and yet few are needed, indeed only one. It is Mary who has chosen the better part, and it is not to be taken from her.' (Luke 10:38–42)

It's tempting to contrast Mary with Martha, contemplation with action, prayer with service. But you can't isolate one passage in the Gospel and forget the others: the story of the Good Samaritan for instance. And still less that the Lord summed up the Law and the Prophets in two equally positive commandments: 'Love God. Love your neighbour.' So what I'm saying is, the ideal thing is to have Martha's hands and Mary's heart.

It's hard to understand how some women – and some men too – can devote their lives to prayer and nothing but prayer, when there are so many things to be done for other people. If God is truly God and truly Father, does he need our prayers? Certainly not because, if we prayed to him less, he would be less God, less powerful, less Father, less good, less perfect.

No, we're the ones who need to pray to God. Since, if we

don't immerse ourselves in the Lord, we forget about our neighbour and then become inhuman ourselves.

I love contemplative religious. They pray on behalf of those who don't know how to pray, who haven't the time or think they haven't the time to pray, and even on behalf of those who don't want to pray because they don't know the Lord. Oh, if only they knew the Lord, they'd be the first to be praying!

I often think if there's any hope for the world – and there really is – we owe it to all these men and woman praying in solitude on behalf of the rest of us.

True, there are self-centred solitudes. I'm not talking about them. I'm thinking of peopled solitudes.

I like often to visit contemplatives. I make a point of bringing them up-to-date on the world situation: 'You mustn't present yourselves alone before the Lord. You've got to carry the whole world in your hands, on your backs.'

I like visiting panoramic view-points. When high above some town, from a skyscraper perhaps, I love looking down on the roofs of the houses. Under each roof are joys or suffering or anguish: 'Lord, on behalf of those who are happy and those who are crushed. . .'

I love a peopled solitude. Peopled by the Lord, peopled by everyone on earth. . .

42

'Do you suppose that I am here to bring peace on earth?
No, I tell you, but rather division. For from now on, a
household of five will be divided: three against two and
two against three; father opposed to son, son to father,
mother to daughter, daughter to mother, mother-in-law to
daughter-in-law, daughter-in-law to mother-in-law.' (Luke
12:51–3)

When we listen to these phrases, we mustn't forget that the
first words announcing the Lord's birth to us were, 'Glory to
Heaven and peace on earth!' and that the last words Christ
spoke were, 'Peace be with you.' Jesus came to teach us what
is essential for peace. He came to say that Almighty God is
the Father of us all.

Nonetheless it's true when we try to live the Gospel, we
often cause or encounter difficulties, even in our own families.
It's true that the Gospel is demanding and we aren't all
always totally determined to live it to its logical conclusions.
Not even in the Church.

Often I smilingly tell my fellow-bishops that we Catholics
– and our Protestant brothers and sisters too for that matter
– are remarkable for the noble statements and resolutions
we produce: but when we have to put life into these noble
resolutions, we run into problems straightaway. Not only with
certain governments and certain privileged groups but also
with one another, within our Church. The Lord warned us:
'I've come to bring the sword, division.'

The last thing we must do is to make these divisions more
rigid. It's always better to convince than to conquer. We must

be patient and do everything we can to march in step with others and not all by ourselves.

If we don't press the absurd claim of being the best, if we present ourselves as brothers and sisters for others, we shall be astounded to discover what a lot of people of good-will there are about. Some of them may perhaps be rather timid, others will be so situated that they can't see things in the same light as we do. But once they come across somebody who speaks from the heart, not seeking to impose anything on them or humiliate them, and not with the conviction of being any cleverer or holier, then they are affected and also join the march.

43

Then he said, 'There was a man who had two sons. The younger one said to his father: "Father, let me have the share of the estate that will come to me." So the father divided the property between them. A few days later, the younger son got together everything he had and left for a distant country where he squandered his money on a life of debauchery.

'When he had spent it all, that country experienced a severe famine, and now he began to feel the pinch; so he hired himself out to one of the local inhabitants who put him on his farm to feed the pigs. And he would willingly have filled himself with the husks the pigs were eating but no one would let him have them. Then he came to his senses and said: "How many of my father's hired men have all the food they want and more, and here am I dying of hunger! I shall leave this place and go to my father and say: Father, I have sinned against heaven and against you; I no longer deserve to be called your son; treat me as one of your hired men." So he left the place and went back to his father.

'While he was still a long way off, his father saw him and was moved with pity. He ran to the boy, clasped him in his arms and kissed him. Then his son said: "Father, I have sinned against heaven and against you. I no longer deserve to be called your son." But the father said to his servants: "Quick! Bring out the best robe and put it on him; put a ring on his finger and sandals on his feet. Bring the calf we have been fattening, and kill it; we will celebrate by having a feast, because this son of mine was dead and has come back to life; he was lost and is found." And they began to celebrate.

'Now the elder son was out in the fields, and on his way back, as he drew near the house, he could hear music and dancing. Calling one of the servants he asked what it was all about. The servant told him: "Your brother has come, and your father has killed the calf we had been fattening because he has got him back safe and sound." He was angry then and refused to go in, and his father came out and began to urge him to come in; but he retorted to his father: "All these years I have slaved for you and never once disobeyed any orders of yours, yet you never offered me so much as a kid for me to celebrate with my friends. But, for this son of yours when he comes back after swallowing up your property – he and his loose women – you kill the calf we had been fattening!"

'The father said: "My son, you are with me always and all I have is yours. But it was only right we should celebrate and rejoice, because your brother here was dead and has come to life; he was lost and is found." ' (Luke 15:11–32)

This is an immortal story. One valid for all time. It tells of the Lord's understanding for human weakness.

One day I was with a mixed group of youngsters. They were talking very freely to me, in the idiom they use today. At one point one of them said, 'You know, Dom Helder, I've been told the Gospel stories. But I've actually lived the story of the Prodigal Son, only in my case I lived it the other way round. It wasn't the son who went off; it was my father, with another woman. Then my mother went off, with another man. . . That's life today, whether you like it or not. We children are the ones who've stayed at home.'

He went on, 'I once heard someone say the prodigal son in the Gospel must have already lost his mother or she would certainly have found some way of persuading him not to leave. But my story's not confined to me. It's a story that keeps on happening; other youngsters know it all too well. My father's living with the mother of one of my mates here now. So what are we to do about it? Deep inside, I want

111

to protest, to rebel. But then I say to myself, "No, it's not Christ's fault." And if in the end I don't judge my father or mother, it's because Christ has taught me human understanding.'

Dear friends, that day I read the parable of the Prodigal Son from a totally new angle. Through the eyes of the child of prodigal parents. It's easy enough to be understanding and kind when we've got everything we need. But what about when we haven't got anything, like this young lad?

There are times when understanding leads us into unlimited indulgence. Sometimes, however, to help our brothers and sisters, love requires us to take a tougher line.

I often come across fathers and mothers in a state of total bewilderment. They are torn between an old, insufficiently nourished, possibly dying love and the hope of new love. I can understand. But before saying, 'I understand', I try to put up a struggle: 'You've no right to do this. Think of your children. Don't think only about yourselves. . .' I try to rouse their sense of responsibility, to remind them of their duties, and I urge them to make the necessary sacrifices entailed. I fight. But eventually, if I'm not understood, it's I who have to understand. The last word, the last way of loving, has to be understanding.

Plainly, we can't be exactly like the Lord; we are only human creatures. But when I ponder on how the Lord loves, I get the feeling that in every case it's different, depending on the individual.

I began thinking this when I was at seminary. I was the librarian. I began by reading the books that appealed to me most, then those I was obliged to read, and finally the rest. Among the rest I spotted the writings and revelations of a number of saints. I read about two dozen of them. I then went to see the man who was much more to me than a Professor of Dogmatic Theology. He was, you might say, my Professor of Life, Professor of Human Understanding. 'Look,' I said, 'I know what these various accounts say isn't the dogma of the Church. I know these saints may have produced these revelations, these confidences ascribed to Christ, out of their own imagination. But I can't bring myself to think they are all made up. So why doesn't Christ say the same thing to each of them?'

My professor smiled: 'My son, we can't measure God's infinite love with our petty human measures.' And he went on to say these remarkable words, 'God loves each man, each woman, in a uniquely individual way.'

I was delighted by this, since it struck me that this was the way I loved too. How upset I used to get when I was little and people asked, 'Which do you love most: Daddy or Mummy?' I loved my father as father and my mother as mother. Differently, but just as much.

It's hard to love like God, sharing out one's love without dividing it, loving each individual without withdrawing any of one's love from the others. We're so grasping. We can only love by devouring. We feel we're being robbed if the person who claims to love us has eyes for others too.

44

'There was a rich man who used to dress in purple and fine linen and feast magnificently every day. And at his gate there used to lie a poor man called Lazarus, covered with sores, who longed to fill himself with what fell from the rich man's table. Even dogs came and licked his sores. Now it happened that the poor man died and was carried away by the angels into Abraham's embrace. The rich man also died and was buried.

'In his torment in Hades he looked up and saw Abraham a long way off with Lazarus in his embrace. So he cried out: "Father Abraham, pity me and send Lazarus to dip the tip of his finger in water and cool my tongue, for I am in agony in these flames." Abraham said: "My son, remember that during your life you had your fill of good things, just as Lazarus his fill of bad. Now he is being comforted here while you are in agony. But that is not all: between us and you a great gulf has been fixed, to prevent those who want to cross from our side to yours or from your side to ours."

'So he said: "Father, I beg you then to send Lazarus to my father's house, since I have five brothers, to give them warning so that they do not come to this place of torment too." Abraham said: "They have Moses and the prophets, let them listen to them." The rich man replied: "Ah no, father Abraham, but if someone comes to them from the dead, they will repent." Then Abraham said to him: "If they will not listen either to Moses or to the prophets, they will not be convinced even if someone should rise from the dead." ' (Luke 16:19–31)

When I listen to this parable I realise that Lazarus-today is the entire 'third world' sitting there at the rich world's gate – that world of countries growing richer and richer. There the 'third world' sits, with its sores, its misery, its hunger.

We think the rich man in the Gospel ought to have invited Lazarus in to a meal: 'Lazarus, Lazarus, come in! There's a chair for you among the guests. You can eat. We can talk. Speak up, Lazarus, say something.'

But, in my experience, when we talk to poor people like that, they still persist in looking on us as masters: 'Yes, boss, yes, boss. . .' – 'Son, I'm not your boss, I'm not your master.' – 'Yes, boss. . .'

It's no easy matter to free the poor from their condition of beggary. The outstretched hand is almost a conditioned reflex. At a good suit, a kind face, a decent house, a nice voice, out comes the hand.

Much needs to be done if we are ever to change the begging syndrome without pushing the poor into hating us, for this would only be to encourage the oppressed of today to become the oppressors of tomorrow.

What we've got to achieve is a world without oppressed or oppressors, but this can't be done by inviting the poor man out there at the gate to sit down at the rich man's table, and then confronting him with dishes he never imagined existed and wines beyond his ken. . .

In Latin America, for the last century and a half, we have experienced political independence without economic independence. So we are well placed to warn our brothers and sisters in Africa and Asia: 'Look out! Those nations that are too powerful, the United States, Russia, China, are bound to have ulterior motives. They help but, in giving, impose their influence. Colonialism will be reborn, brothers. In a different form, but it will be colonialism just the same.'

My dream for our Latin America and for the other continents being crushed, is a genuine economic integration without external or internal colonialism either of left or right. Allowing Lazarus to talk to the rich man, man to man, as human creature to human creature, as child of God to child of God. Allowing true dialogue, true sharing, in a world without domination.

45

Some Pharisees approached him, and to put him to the test they said, 'Is it against the Law for a man to divorce his wife on any pretext whatever?' He answered, 'Have you not read that the Creator from the beginning made them male and female and that he said: This is why a man leaves his father and mother and becomes attached to his wife, and the two become one flesh? They are no longer two, therefore, but one flesh. So then, what God has united, human beings must not divide.'

They said to him, 'Then why did Moses command that a writ of dismissal should be given in cases of divorce?' He said to them, 'It was because you were so hard-hearted, that Moses allowed you to divorce your wives, but it was not like this from the beginning. Now I say this to you: anyone who divorces his wife – I am not speaking of an illicit marriage – and marries another, is guilty of adultery.' (Matt. 19:3–9)

When the Lord laid down this very strict law about the indissolubility of marriage, he said in reply to the question about what Moses had commanded, 'This was because you were so hard-hearted.' I think our hard-heartedness needs honest and courageous examination.

The Lord walks with his people. He keeps us company. He listens to us. He assesses our weaknesses. Today, too, he understands the complexities and strains of the times. Personally, I am quite certain we churchmen ought to be Christ's living presence among his people, we ought to have the guts to ask ourselves in such complex times as these whether a more generous approach and understanding might not in certain cases be right and appropriate.

I know you may say, 'But even today marriage is still a sacrament. Our Lord affords all the help required by the sacrament, of which both parties are the ministers.' But, I insist, we shepherds ought to have the guts to see the difficulties as they are.

'But what about the children?' you object. I know. I come across many children of divorcees. I know the sort of dramas they have to live through. But when a couple reach the point of tearing one another apart or of even coming to blows, this too is not the most helpful of scenarios for children to grow up in.

No, the whole problem needs to be re-examined. And Christ's words can help us to do it. He speaks of hard-heartedness. I think he understands and is inviting us to understand the strains and difficulties of our times.

Some forty years ago, a great, world-famous painter decorated a chapel at Belo Horizonte. He painted a figure of St Francis. Now, this St Francis was enormous, a giant. And one of his legs was painted like an anatomical study, fleshless with the nerves, muscles and bones exposed. The bishop put the chapel under an interdict. He assumed the painter must be anti-religious, anti-clerical, even a communist, and that he had intended to ridicule the saints of the Church.

One day some of our bishops met to inspect the chapel and decide whether the interdict should be maintained. I wasn't a bishop then, but I went with them. They saw from my expression that I didn't approve of the interdict. They questioned me and this is what I said:

'This, in all simplicity, is what I think. Artists, sharers in God's creative power, have antennae. They can pick up the hopes and agonies of the world. In a world as disturbed as ours, we haven't the right to expect musicians to create very harmonious compositions. The same goes for painting. Artists are immersed in a world of strains, injustices, dislocations, violence. . .' – 'But why paint St Francis as a giant?' – 'Because he is a giant and we are pygmies. That's exactly what St Francis is. The painter has grasped the very truth about St Francis.' – 'But what about this leg with no skin?

Is he making fun of Francis of Assisi?' – 'No, the painter clearly saw it isn't an easy life being a saint. Holiness exacts a price. Often walls collapse, wounds open, you lose your skin. Honestly, it's no easy life being a saint.'

And like artists, we shepherds need antennae too. We need to feel, we need to understand. This doesn't mean we have to justify everything. But nor does it mean we have to condemn. We aren't judges. We need to have antennae to understand, and we ought to do everything we can to improve that sacred institution, the family.

46

He was setting out on a journey when a man ran up, knelt before him and put this question to him, 'Good master, what must I do to inherit eternal life?' Jesus said to him, 'Why do you call me good? No one is good but God alone. You know the commandments: You shall not kill; You shall not commit adultery; You shall not steal; You shall not give false witness; You shall not defraud; Honour your father and mother.' And he said to him, 'Master, I have kept all these since my earliest days.' Jesus looked steadily at him and he was filled with love for him, and he said, 'You need to do one thing more. Go and sell what you own and give the money to the poor, and you will have treasure in heaven; then come, follow me.' But his face fell at these words and he went away sad, for he was a man of great wealth.

Jesus looked round and said to his disciples, 'How hard it is for those who have riches to enter the kingdom of God! The disciples were astounded by these words, but Jesus insisted, 'My children,' he said to them, 'how hard it is to enter the kingdom of God! It is easier for a camel to pass through the eye of a needle than for someone rich to enter the kingdom of God.' They were more astonished than ever, saying to one another, 'In that case, who can be saved?' Jesus gazed at them and said, 'By human resources it is impossible, but not for God because for God everything is possible.' (Mark 10:17–27)

What Jesus has to tell us about money is very serious, very grave.

Money in itself we regard as morally indifferent, neutral. With money one can do either good or evil. Even so, money can change us. We think we own it, but it can very easily own us.

Good heavens! Once people start trying to make a profit, they lose all sense of moderation. They keep on wanting more.

And yet, in the most critical of moments, money cannot be a faithful friend. It's often my lot to be present when poor people are dying and when rich people are dying. The poor have their worries, their sufferings. They imagine that, if they had money, they could call in the doctor and buy medicines. The rich have everything. They're surrounded with medical experts summoned from far away, who consult one another, deliver their opinions, prescribe treatments and instal extremely expensive equipment. But once the hour of death arrives, all this is instantly useless, totally useless.

At the cemetery, the poor often don't even have coffins. They are laid directly in the ground. The rich have coffins, family vaults, wreaths. But for rich and poor alike, once below ground, the dialogue with the worms is the same. And the dialogue with the worms is the least of it. If we truly believe in eternal life, we know the only thing we take with us is the good we have done during our lives.

Often people spend their lives, at the cost of great self-sacrifice, struggling to make money for the sake of their children. But when death draws near, it isn't hard to imagine the arguments breaking out among these children over the inventory and will. I've known the most united of families quarrel and split into factions at a death if there's any money about.

And many, many women whose husbands devote their lives to money-making come to me and say, 'Dom Helder, I'd rather a thousand times not have the luxuries we've got and still have my husband's love. I've got everything you can imagine, but the most important thing of all is missing. I need my husband's love. And I'm losing that the faster the money rolls in.'

47

'Now the kingdom of Heaven is like a landowner going out at daybreak to hire workers for his vineyard. He made an agreement with the workers for one denarius a day and sent them to his vineyard. Going out at about the third hour he saw others standing idle in the market place and said to them: 'You go to my vineyard too and I will give you a fair wage.' So they went. At about the sixth hour and again at about the ninth hour, he went out and did the same. Then at about the eleventh hour he went out and found more men standing around, and he said to them: "Why have you been standing here idle all day?" – "Because no one has hired us," they answered. He said to them: "You go into my vineyard too."

'In the evening, the owner of the vineyard said to his bailiff: "Call the workers and pay them their wages, starting with the last arrivals and ending with the first." So those who were hired at about the eleventh hour came forward and received one denarius each. When the first came, they expected to get more, but they too received one denarius each. They took it, but grumbled at the landowner saying: "The men who came last have done only one hour, and you have treated them the same as us, though we have done a heavy day's work in all the heat." He answered one of them and said: "My friend, I am not being unjust to you; did we not agree on one denarius? Take your earnings and go. I choose to pay the lastcomer as much as I pay you. Have I no right to do what I like with my own? Why should you be envious because I am generous?" – Thus the last will be first, and the first, last. (For many are called, but few are chosen.)' (Matt. 20:1–16)

This parable certainly isn't meant to be a lesson in economics. In countries like mine which have large numbers of labourers out of work, it's very tempting for employers to impose their own terms by playing off one against the other: 'If you don't agree to my rates of pay, no problem! There are dozens, hundreds, outside only hoping for that.' No, Christ's teaching taken as a whole shows the parable isn't a lesson in economics, but a lesson about the spiritual life: you can gain in one second what you haven't deserved over any number of years, possibly even over a lifetime.

The story makes me think of the man known as the 'good thief'. For him to have been on a cross, next to Christ, no doubt he had done some pretty terrible things in the course of his life. His mate, the one known as the 'bad thief', kept hurling his taunts at Jesus: 'If you've done such a lot of miracles, save yourself and take us with you.' But the 'good thief' had the honesty and humility to say, 'You and I deserve to be here. But he doesn't. He's different from us, he's good. . . . Lord, remember me when you come into your kingdom.' These few words were enough. The Lord didn't say, 'Thank you for the kind thought. In a few years' time when you've atoned for your life, which hasn't been by any means exemplary, I'll admit you.' No, he said, 'This day you will be with me. This very day.'

Isn't that fantastic! One second of good-will, of perfection, of grace received and lived, can be worth a whole lifetime.

This isn't easily grasped by people who have worked their guts out trying to live their entire lives according to the rules. As in the parable about the prodigal son's elder brother, the Lord invites us, the 'faithful ones', to understand the feelings of the shepherd who makes such a fuss of the sheep once lost, now found – to share his joy, instead of shutting ourselves away in rebellious envy.

48

When the other ten heard this they were indignant with the two brothers. But Jesus called them to him and said, 'You know that among the gentiles the rulers lord it over them, and great men make their authority felt. Among you this is not to happen. No; anyone who wants to become great among you must be your servant, and anyone who wants to be first among you must be your slave, just as the Son of man came not to be served but to serve, and to give his life as a ransom for many.' (Matt. 20:24–8)

During the Second Vatican Council, much was said about 'a Church serving and poor'. This was essentially concerned with the Church in relation to money and with its external signs of wealth. More serious however than the temptation posed by money is the one presented by prestige and power.

Sad to say, we have forgotten Christ's words: 'I didn't come to be served but to serve.' A Church serving and poor. . . It's easy enough to call ourselves – as the Holy Father does – the servant of God's servants. But have we opted, once and for all, to serve? I say again: the temptation of prestige and power is strong, very strong.

A Church serving and poor. A Church that is servant of the poor. Opting for the poor doesn't mean spurning the rich. We have no right to spurn, not even to forget about, anybody. Why then this preference for the poor? The rich often consider they don't need us. In a brotherly way and without judging, still less condemning them, we ought to help them open their eyes, their ears, their consciences. But they make no demands on us. The poor, the oppressed, on the other hand, really do need us – cost us what that may.

Serving and poor, servant of the poor. I never get tired of repeating this: to do justice is the greatest love in our deplorably unjust times. And the greatest poverty for the Church is to consent to be misjudged, to risk its reputation, to lose its prestige. To be treated as subversives, revolutionaries, communists perhaps: that's our poverty, the poverty Jesus asks of his Church in the age we're living in now.

49

Mary went to Jesus, and as soon as she saw him she threw herself at his feet, saying, 'Lord, if you had been here, my brother would not have died.' At the sight of her tears, and those of the Jews who had come with her, Jesus was greatly distressed, and with a profound sigh he said, 'Where have you put him?' They said, 'Lord, come and see.' Jesus wept; and the Jews said, 'See how much he loved him!' But there were some who remarked, 'He opened the eyes of the blind man. Could he not have prevented this man's death?'

Sighing again, Jesus reached the tomb: it was a cave with a stone to close the opening. Jesus said, 'Take the stone away.' Martha, the dead man's sister, said to him, 'Lord, by now he will smell; this is the fourth day since he died.' Jesus replied, 'Have I not told you that if you believe you will see the glory of God?' So they took the stone away. Then Jesus lifted up his eyes and said: 'Father, I thank you for hearing my prayer. I myself knew that you hear me always, but I speak for the sake of all these who are standing around me, so that they may believe it was you who sent me.'

When he had said this, he cried in a loud voice, 'Lazarus, come out!' The dead man came out, his feet and hands bound with strips of material, and a cloth over his face. Jesus said to them, 'Unbind him, let him go free.' (John 11:32–44)

It's good to be told that Christ was distressed and wept too. We have a real duty to share in our neighbours', in our brothers' and sisters', sufferings and joys.

I remember a young man who was obviously at the point of death. I was sitting beside him with his family. He took my hands and said, 'Father, if you will it, death will go away. Yes,' he insisted, 'the Lord has said so. If you have faith you can do the impossible. Even with a tiny bit of faith you can order mountains to throw themselves into the sea. You do have faith, help me. God! Tell me to get up.'

I thought: he's right. . . If with all my faith I gave the command, not in my name but in Christ's, he would get up, he would recover his health. . . But then I thought: perhaps the Lord knows this would be too much for my humility. . . Oh, how weak we are! How much stronger our faith still has to grow, before it can outweigh our misgivings! . . . All I did was to sit there, saying nothing. . . . Tuberculosis often produces a feverish death-agony. He was agitated, distressed. I thought it wiser to leave the Lord to speak to him in his heart.

Once he was dead, I said to the family, 'Now I can speak. I've been praying in silence, but don't be misled. Don't imagine that death has been the victor this morning. You remember what André Malraux said to Charles de Gaulle: "That's death – death always wins in the end"? No, that's a delusion. From the depths of my heart and with total conviction, I assure you: this is only your son's, your brother's, body. His spirit is with the Lord. And even this body, which we shall soon be carrying to the grave, will come back to life, we shall meet it again, one day. Death doesn't have the last word. Christ has risen from the dead. We too shall rise again. Of that I assure you. But I must also confess, when I was asked to work a miracle – although I knew that Christ would be working it and that, if with all my faith I were to ask him, the miracle would have taken place – I didn't dare. I couldn't be certain about my humility. There, now I have confessed.'

50

Six days before the Passover, Jesus went to Bethany, where
Lazarus was, whom he had raised from the dead. They
gave a dinner for him there; Martha waited on them and
Lazarus was among those at table. Mary brought in a
pound of very costly ointment, pure nard, and with it
anointed the feet of Jesus, wiping them with her hair; the
house was filled with the scent of the ointment. Then Judas
Iscariot – one of his disciples, the man who was to betray
him – said, 'Why was this ointment not sold for three
hundred denarii and the money given to the poor?' He said
this, not because he cared about the poor, but because he
was a thief; he was in charge of the common fund and used
to help himself to the contents. So Jesus said, 'Leave her
alone; let her keep it for the day of my burial. You have
the poor with you always, you will not always have me.'
(John 12:1–8)

Some of Christ's sayings are shockingly exploited. For
instance: 'The poor you will always have with you.' People
even go so far as to justify, not only poverty, but physical
misery, injustice and oppression on the strength of this
'always, there will always be the poor'. Sometimes during my
'vigils' I make bold to say, 'Ah, Lord, you know what you
have to say. But look how people exploit what you do say!'

In this episode however, there's also the story of Mary.
Her gesture reminds me of a woman, a lady who often used
to bring me money or things she let me sell for the poor. One
day she brought me some scent: 'I've been given this scent
as a present. I don't know the first thing about perfume but

I'm told it's very rare, very dear, incredibly expensive. Dom Helder, I've had an idea. This time I'm asking you not to sell the scent. If you can do it, I should like you to take it to some lonely place. And there, since you are a priest and your mission is to offer sacrifice, I should like you to break the bottle and let the perfume escape as an act of worship to the Creator, to the Father, on behalf of all those who never think of worshipping or have no wish to worship him, on behalf of the whole human race.'

I was delighted. I made a good 'vigil'. I found a lonely place where there were some stones. And then, in the true spirit of offering, I broke the bottle. How wonderful it was! In amazement, I discovered what a perfume of great price was really like.

Next day, the lady came to see me again. 'Dom Helder,' she said, 'I'm feeling a little uneasy. The fact is, I think it was vain of me to let you into my little secret. I could have broken that bottle myself. Perhaps I was being vain in wanting you to know that I too was capable of making a gesture. . . How weak we are, Dom Helder.' I said, 'Having the humility to acknowledge this trace of what may be vanity is a pretty important thing in itself.'

I also often think about people who, like Judas but fortunately for other reasons, are shocked by the amount of money spent on cathedrals, churches, church plate and so forth, when there are so many poor people to be helped.

However, in my experience, the poor in our poorer districts are by no means backward in wanting their churches to be beautiful: 'The Believers (here that means the Protestants) have a beautiful church. We ought to have a beautiful one as well!' Similarly, the Blacks want beautiful churches for the Blacks, possibly because they don't get a very warm welcome in those belonging to the Whites.

Naturally I say, 'Dear friends, forgive me, but you do know the Lord isn't all that desperate for churches. He's present everywhere. The whole universe is his house. We walk within the Lord.'

It's we human creatures who need churches. And the Lord smiles, knowing our weakness. We are so blind, so deaf, that we forget we're living in the Lord and that the Lord is living in us.

Then I remind them once again that each individual is a living temple for the Lord. As long as there are human creatures needing to be built up, to be set upright, to be restored, to be set free, it's on these – these living churches – that we ought to concentrate.

But sometimes they go on insisting: 'Even if we are living in misery, even if we haven't got homes, we want a church, a beautiful church. And that will be our home.'

That's when I have to give in. And I have to make sure the church won't be only the home of the faithful at the times of mass, the sacraments and public prayer but everyone else's home too, open to the needs of all, a communal home where all can meet to express and share their joys and sorrows and encourage one another on their journey.

51

Then the Pharisees went away to work out between them how to trap him in what he said. And they sent their disciples to him, together with some Herodians, to say, 'Master, we know that you are not afraid of anyone, because human rank means nothing to you. Give us your opinion, then. Is it permissible to pay taxes to Caesar or not?' But Jesus was aware of their malice and replied, 'You hypocrites! Why are you putting me to the test? Show me the money you pay the tax with.' They handed him a denarius, and he said, 'Whose portrait is this? Whose title?' They replied, 'Caesar's.' Then he said to them, 'Very well, pay Caesar what belongs to Caesar – and God what belongs to God.' When they heard this they were amazed; they left him alone and went away. (Matt. 22:15–22)

Here is another of those passages that can be read, and is often used, in a different and opposite sense from what was intended.

I'm not a textual critic. I don't propose to argue over this passage. I know there are plenty of other sayings of Jesus helping us to grasp the totality of what he meant to say, not merely throwing light on a part of it. I also know that the Church goes on being the living presence of Christ. With all respect for what the Lord said in the days of the apostles, I try to keep alert and catch what he's saying today. And I sense that Christ does not intend to separate, to set up an antithesis between, God and human beings, spiritual values and temporal realities, eternity and our duties of today. Eternity begins here and now. Here and now we're building it.

People will always argue the respective merits of 'horizon-talism' and 'verticalism', of 'evangelisation' and 'humanisation'. I'm certain the Lord doesn't see these as separate, still less as mutually opposed. God's history and human history are interwoven. They proceed together.

Personally speaking, I could never confine myself solely to 'evangelisation'. For some years, as you know, the authorities in my country prohibited me from appearing on television. At a given moment, I was informed I might speak on TV again if I stuck strictly to evangelisation. I replied that as far as I was concerned it would be absolutely impossible for me to draw the line. To those who waste their time discussing the respective merits of 'horizontalism' and 'verticalism', I always say: neither the horizontal line alone, nor the vertical line alone, can form a cross. To have a proper cross, you have to have both the horizontal and the vertical. The horizontal line is the arms of Christ spread wide to all humanity's huge problems.

Oh, I don't care for those representations of Christ on the cross where he has his arms above his head. I like to see him with his arms wide open, since this is how I always meet him, always ready to accept and bear all the facts of human life. The Passion still goes on. I touch, I encounter the Passion every minute of my life. And Christ is there, with open arms.

During my life as a priest and bishop, I have seen and experienced several kinds of relationship between what used to be called 'the two swords': the temporal power and the spiritual power, State and Church. At one point I even thought we in Brazil had struck an ideal balance of relations, based on mutual respect and effective co-operation. The chariot of the Church and the chariot of the State advanced in tandem, solidly linked together. And this with the best intentions in the world, since we thought we could work together like this in the service of our people.

But today I am calmly convinced that the Church's only engagement and solidarity should be with the people. If the government too becomes engaged with the people, then a fruitful meeting between Government and Church can take place at this level.

But governments, whether of right or left, who claim they

131

wish to serve the people, do not care to meet the Church with the people. They are happy enough to load the Church with honours and privileges, provided it stays inside its churches, praising God with lovely services – provided it doesn't meddle in current problems. Economic, social, political problems are Earth's business, not the Kingdom of Heaven's!

We cannot accept this position, the role of a museum-church. It isn't a question of reclaiming power or of seeking to recover the prestige that goes with that power. It's a question of doing our brotherly, or sisterly, duty by our fellow-beings under ordeal, suffering, being crushed. We are responsible for being brother or sister to all people without stopping to consider whether we're dealing with Catholics, or Christians or believers. Enough for us to know that every human creature is our brother or our sister, the child of the same Father.

52

Some Sadducees – those who argue that there is no resurrection – approached him and they put this question to
him, 'Master, Moses prescribed for us, if a man's married
brother dies childless, the man must marry the widow to
raise up children for his brother. Well then, there were
seven brothers; the first, having married a wife, died childless. The second and then the third married the widow.
And the same with all seven, they died leaving no children.
Finally the woman herself died. Now, at the resurrection,
whose wife will she be, since she had been married to all
seven?'

Jesus replied, 'The children of this world take wives and
husbands, but those who are judged worthy of a place in
the other world and in the resurrection from the dead do
not marry because they can no longer die, for they are the
same as the angels, and being children of the resurrection
they are children of God. And Moses himself implies that
the dead rise again, in the passage about the bush where
he calls the Lord the God of Abraham, the God of Isaac
and the God of Jacob. Now he is God, not of the dead, but
of the living; for to him everyone is alive.' (Luke 20:27–38)

First of all I should like to tell you about my reactions when
very close friends of mine express grave doubts about the
after-life or maintain that death is the end of everything.

I don't enjoy and am not good at arguing. But I am utterly
convinced that human beings have hungers and thirsts that
can never be completely appeased here on earth. Hunger for
truth, hunger for beauty, hunger for goodness, for the

absolute, for the infinite, for the eternal. We aren't earth-worms. When I am on the beach and see the waves rising, breaking and vanishing back into the sea, I feel, I know, that we aren't waves. I don't know how to prove this. When I was studying philosophy, I was taught the five ways of demonstrating the existence of God. I didn't catch on very well: why did anyone need to demonstrate God's existence? It seemed transparently obvious to me that the Lord is there. It seems to me equally obvious that we are designed for eternity.

People wonder how the resurrection can be possible. How will it happen? Will an angel really sound a trumpet in the graveyards?

I've never had any problem over the resurrection. I say, 'Look, friend, this body, your body now, the one I'm looking at, isn't the body you had in your cradle, it isn't the one your school-friends used to know, it isn't the one that went to university. How many times has your body changed already, or will again completely change in the future? But you are always the same person. Since, inside your various bodies, there is one absolutely personal, unifying factor.'

Or again I say, 'Here's a piece of fruit. You eat half and the fruit becomes you. I eat the other half and the same fruit becomes me. The same fruit. . .'

I realise these arguments aren't particularly good ones. But this is my way of stating my conviction that, within us, we each have a living spirit. When death comes, this living spirit survives.

And one day, when the Lord sees good, this living spirit will retake shape, retake body, in some way we cannot imagine, any more than a newborn child can imagine the kind of body it will have at twenty. But we shall recognise one another. Eternity would be unacceptable, unnatural, if, having known and recognised and loved one another on this earth, we weren't to know and recognise and love one another on the new earth, in the new heaven.

53

Before the festival of the Passover, Jesus, knowing that his hour had come to pass from this world to the Father, having loved those who were his in the world, loved them to the end.

They were at supper, and the devil had already put it into the mind of Judas Iscariot, son of Simon, to betray him. Jesus knew that the Father had put everything into his hands, and that he had come from God and was returning to God, and he got up from table, removed his outer garments and, taking a towel, wrapped it round his waist; he then poured water into a basin and began to wash the disciples' feet and to wipe them with the towel he was wearing.

He came to Simon Peter, who said to him, 'Lord, are you going to wash my feet?' Jesus answered, 'At the moment you do not know what I am doing, but later you will understand.' 'Never!' said Peter, 'You shall never wash my feet.' Jesus replied, 'If I do not wash you, you can have no share with me.' Simon Peter said, 'Well then, Lord, not only my feet, but my hands and my head as well!' Jesus said, 'No one who has had a bath needs washing, such a person is clean all over. You too are clean, though not all of you are.' He knew who was going to betray him, and that was why he said, 'though not all of you are'.

When he had washed their feet and put on his outer garments again he went back to the table. 'Do you understand', he said, 'what I have done to you? You call me Master and Lord, and rightly; so I am. If I, then, the Lord and Master, have washed your feet, you must wash each other's feet. I have given you an example so that you may copy what I have done to you.' (John 13:1–15)

Every Maundy Thursday before celebrating the Eucharist, we hold a beautiful ceremony; there is always an enormous congregation to see the bishop or priest washing twelve people's feet. Thus we call to mind what the Lord himself did.

However I always feel a little uneasy when I see our twelve apostles offering themselves with their feet already well washed. The message ought to be: 'Dear brothers and sisters, we aren't here today to mime the washing of feet already carefully washed. We're here to tell you we're ready to behave as flesh-and-blood brothers should, ready to help one another and do for our brothers and sisters what is really necessary for them, what they truly need.'

Otherwise, religion is in danger of being a mere theatrical spectacle. Religion has to be lived, not merely acted. The Lord set us an example that evening, as throughout his life. If we Christians had set an example of always being readier to serve than to be served, the world would already be a better place.

And then, there's Judas. We often have the feeling of meeting Judases on our path – Judases willing to settle for less than thirty pieces of silver. But the Judases of yesterday and the Judases of today: to what extent are they really answerable for their actions? True, the Lord said, 'It would be better if he hadn't ever been born.'

But I, for my part, hope the Lord's mercy won't make an exception of the Judases throughout the ages. This helps me when I run across one. One day somebody spat in my face. Not easy to stomach. Our very nature protests and shudders. . . But it's easier when you think what the Lord put up with. Everything's easier then.

54

And as they were eating he took bread, and when he had said the blessing he broke it and gave it to them. 'Take it,' he said, 'this is my body.' Then he took a cup, and when he had given thanks he handed it to them, and all drank from it, and he said to them, 'This is my blood, the blood of the covenant, poured out for many. In truth I tell you, I shall never drink wine any more until the day I drink the new wine in the kingdom of God.' (Mark 14:22–5)

At mass, during the consecration, it's always a matter of amazement to me, how the priest can survive that extraordinary moment. It's so overpowering for us, so far beyond the human dimension, seeing the Son of God come down into our hands, having him there before our eyes, actually holding him. How can we support this immense weight? . . . And what riches to offer to the Father! 'Lord, you can now demand the infinite of us. We owe you the infinite. The infinite you give us; we offer it to you.'

The mass is wonderful, and it is wonderful to know that the bread I receive and the bread I give is truly the Lord Jesus and truly our food. He was already within us as great God. He is now within us in his human nature, by giving us his body to eat.

What is also wonderful is that the mass embraces the whole day. Everything becomes an offering. I don't go through the day with my arms and hands raised, as at the altar; people wouldn't understand and would take me for a lunatic. But, spiritually speaking, this is how I go about the business of the day, offering up the joys and sorrows, hopes and fears, virtues and weaknesses, everything I see or hear or imagine or dream.

It's also true that after the consecration we find no difficulty in believing that everything around us, everything, comes from the Creator or from humanity the co-creator. There is nothing, absolutely nothing, that isn't alive and holy.

As for making one's communion: this isn't only receiving Christ. In receiving Christ we embrace the entire human race. If, when communicating, I say, 'Lord, with you I receive everyone, with one single exception . . . and that one, well, I really must draw the line at that. . .' – this isn't a true communion. Communion presupposes that our hearts have really assumed the infinite dimensions of Christ's heart. People of every race, of every age, of every creed, of every aspiration, of every sin, are taken up in Christ to the last one of them, and taken up in the Christian in communion. This is the Christian's joy and responsibility and, in a special manner, the priest's.

55

He then left to make his way as usual to the Mount of Olives, with the disciples following. When he reached the place he said to them, 'Pray not to be put to the test.'

Then he withdrew from them, about a stone's throw away, and knelt down and prayed. 'Father, he said, 'if you are willing, take this cup away from me. Nevertheless, let your will be done, not mine.' Then an angel appeared to him, coming from heaven to give him strength. In his anguish he prayed even more earnestly, and his sweat fell to the ground like great drops of blood.

When he rose from prayer he went to the disciples and found them sleeping for sheer grief. And he said to them, 'Why are you asleep? Get up and pray not to be put to the test.' (Luke 22:39–46)

We often forget that the Son of God, true God like the Father and the Holy Spirit, is also true human being, like any other human creature. Here we see the Son of God experiencing very human fear. I love this passage. It's encouraging. It shows that we too have a right to be afraid, to be weak.

You know, no one can foretell how he will react to pain or torture. In my experience those who appear the toughest beforehand are the ones who sometimes turn out to be weaker. The ones who stand firm are often the ones who were afraid, who had no faith in themselves.

We are not born for pain or death. We are born for life and joy.

I can also grasp that in Christ's agony there was not only the anguish of physical pain and approaching death. There was also the vision of the world and the world's sins: self-centredness in particular, which is the greatest sin of all, and the consequences flowing from self-centredness. He saw that, his sacrifice notwithstanding, self-centredness would go on crushing thousands on thousands of millions of human creatures.

I don't underplay the human fear of martyrdom, but there was also his terrible sadness as God's envoy.

56

Pilate then had Jesus taken away and scourged; and after this, the soldiers twisted some thorns into a crown and put it on his head and dressed him in a purple robe. They kept coming up to him and saying, 'Hail, king of the Jews!', and slapping him in the face.

Pilate came outside again and said to them, 'Look, I am going to bring him out to you to let you see that I find no case against him.' Jesus then came out wearing the crown of thorns and the purple robe. Pilate said, 'Here is the man.' When they saw him, the chief priests and the guards shouted, 'Crucify him! Crucify him!' Pilate said, 'Take him yourselves and crucify him: I find no case against him.' The Jews replied, 'We have a Law, and according to that Law he ought to be put to death, because he has claimed to be Son of God.'

When Pilate heard them say this his fears increased. Re-entering the Praetorium, he said to Jesus, 'Where do you come from?' But Jesus made no answer. Pilate then said to him, 'Are you refusing to speak to me? Surely you know I have power to release you and I have power to crucify you?' Jesus replied, 'You would have no power over me at all if it had not been given you from above; that is why the one who handed me over to you has the greater guilt.'

From that moment Pilate was anxious to set him free, but the Jews shouted, 'If you set him free you are no friend of Caesar's; anyone who makes himself king is defying Caesar.' Hearing these words, Pilate had Jesus brought out, and seated him on the chair of judgement at a place called the Pavement, in Hebrew Gabbatha. It was the Day of Preparation, about the sixth hour. 'Here is your king,' said Pilate to the Jews. But they shouted, 'Away with him, away with him, crucify him.' Pilate said, 'Shall I crucify your king?' The chief priests answered, 'We have no king except Caesar.' So at that Pilate handed him over to them to be crucified.' (John 19:1–16)

I have the impression Pilate was a decent man, but of that brand of decency often encountered down the centuries, which is one of the cruellest scourges to afflict humanity: a decency which is alloyed with weakness and without the guts to proclaim and stand up for justice.

'I know all about justice. This man is innocent. I find nothing against him' – 'You may not find anything against him. But don't forget, you're the governor and you're going to lose your job!' For here comes the conclusive argument: 'He says he's a king, and those who claim to be kings are Caesar's enemies.'

Often we assume that Christ died solely for claiming to be the Son of God. But I think there were two factors. He did claim to be the Son of God and this shocked the high priests of Jewry. But he also proclaimed himself to be a king, and this was subversion against the governor, hence against Caesar.

I'm not passing judgement on Pilate but thinking rather of the very large family of the Pilates, of Pilatism, of the decency that keeps quiet because it has no guts.

I don't pass judgement on Pilate. I know it's easier to be brave or to put up a show of being brave, when one is comparatively free, when one has no family responsibilities.

But things are bad here. On our continent, it's easy for us to get accused of being subversives and communists, when we try to stand up for the human rights of those who are being crushed. Many, many people know we are neither subversives nor communists. Why don't they say anything? Why don't they speak up and defend us?

But the point also has to be grasped: many people aren't in the kind of position that allows them to be brave or to make a stand. We have to grasp this and put up with being misjudged.

57

Joseph of Arimathaea, who was a disciple of Jesus – though a secret one because he was afraid of the Jews – asked Pilate to let him remove the body of Jesus. Pilate gave permission, so they came and took it away. Nicodemus came as well – the same one who had first come to Jesus at night-time – and he brought a mixture of myrrh and aloes, weighing about a hundred pounds. They took the body of Jesus and bound it in linen cloths with the spices, following the Jewish burial custom. At the place where he had been crucified there was a garden, and in this garden a new tomb in which no one had yet been buried. Since it was the Jewish Day of Preparation and the tomb was nearby, they laid Jesus there. (John 19:38–42)

What about the Holy Shroud of Turin, preserving the image of the crucified Christ? How does this affect you?

People who take an interest in historic objects of this sort are, in my opinion, quite entitled to do so. But I hold the Lord in my hands every morning. I lay him on a piece of linen called a corporal. Every day I have his shroud. . .

Agreed, but if the Shroud of Turin is genuine, it does at least show what human features Christ took while he was alive on earth.

However true a picture of Christ's face it may be, in my opinion you can't detect any reflections of his divinity in it. I admire people who devote their efforts to painting or sculpting Christ, his eyes, his lips, his hands. . . But more important than his physical features is the divine light radiating through them. But then again, forgive me for repeating myself, the living Christ is here, today, with me. . .

Whenever I say mass, I can almost hear the Father looking at me and saying, 'This is my beloved Son.' And so I myself can say, 'Brothers and sisters, now we are with the living Christ. We can say the prayer which he himself has taught us, which he can say with us, which he loves saying with us. For he too says, Our Father. . .'

What do you think about that timid disciple, Joseph of Arimathaea?

What moves me is the Lord's kindness in accepting timorous disciples. 'I should like to visit you but I'm afraid to. I'm not brave enough to come in the daytime. I'll wait till the evening, after nightfall. And might we perhaps meet somewhere else, not at your house, somewhere where we shan't be seen together?' I've got friends like that. Sometimes I feel like saying, 'If you haven't the guts to take risks for a friend, go away.' But I remind myself that the Lord was prepared to have frightened friends. He understood them. He was even prepared to hand his body over after death to one of these frightened friends. What about that for an example of understanding and generosity!

58

Mary was standing outside near the tomb, weeping. Then, as she wept, she stooped to look inside, and saw two angels in white sitting where the body of Jesus had been, one at the head, the other at the feet. They said, 'Woman, why are you weeping?' 'They have taken my Lord away,' she replied, 'and I don't know where they have put him.' As she said this she turned round and saw Jesus standing there, though she did not realise that it was Jesus. Jesus said to her, 'Woman, why are you weeping? Who are you looking for?' Supposing him to be the gardener, she said, 'Sir, if you have taken him away, tell me where you have put him, and I will go and remove him.' Jesus said, 'Mary!' She turned round then and said to him in Hebrew, 'Rabbuni!' – which means Master. Jesus said to her, 'Do not cling to me, because I have not yet ascended to the Father. But go and find my brothers, and tell them: I am ascending to my Father and your Father, to my God and your God.' So Mary of Magdala told the disciples, 'I have seen the Lord,' and that he had said these things to her. (John 20:11–18)

I like to think of Mary Magdalen as the apostle to the apostles – like the Samaritan woman, whose mission was to lead the Samaritans to Christ. But in this instance it's more significant, since it's to proclaim the resurrection. This ought to be a corrective to the way we pass judgement on sinners of both sexes.

But knowing how much Mary Magdalen loved the Lord, it's hard to understand why-she couldn't recognise him right-away. She actually thought he was the gardener. It was the same too with the disciples who met the risen Christ on the way to Emmaus. They had lived with the Lord for three years. When you love somebody, you can recognise them by their voice or even by the way they walk. But no, they walked and talked with him and still they couldn't recognise him. Until he shared the loaf with them.

I was thinking about this one day when someone knocked on my door. It was a poor man. He had interrupted my meditation on the disciples at Emmaus: how was it they hadn't been able to recognise Christ? To get rid of the fellow as quickly as I could, I gave him a little cash, a smile and good-bye. But the moment the door was shut, I realised: 'You've behaved exactly like the disciples at Emmaus. The Lord Jesus knocked on your door, he spoke to you, and you couldn't get rid of the living Christ fast enough to return to your thoughts on the blindness of your brothers, the disciples of Emmaus.'

Often too, when reading the story of the disciples at Emmaus, I think of the responsibility we owe to those who are perhaps at the gates of despair. Our door, on which they knock, for them may be the last. They ask and they listen perhaps for the last time. It's important to have time to spare for people who, like the disciples at Emmaus, have reached the gates of despair.

Oh, what a grace, Lord, it would be, to be transparent to the living Christ within us! And to remember that the disciples of Emmaus recognised Christ the moment he broke the loaf. When I say mass and break the bread, I always think of the Lord's ingenuity in this.

I remember a woman who had, one day, persuaded her father to go with her to mass. Her father was a very important person. He had lost his faith. So she prayed: 'Lord, Lord, transfigure yourself during mass. My father's here. Touch his heart.' When the mass was over, she was anxious to find out whether his eyes had been opened, whether the Eucharist had touched his heart. But what he came out with was a fearful indictment of us priests, of us the faithful. 'My girl,' he said, 'that lot don't believe Christ *is* in the Eucharist.'

Now of course we mustn't overdo things. The Lord doesn't

146

care for extremes. But it is important that we should partici-
pate more truly, more nearly, in the celebration of Christ. So
that everyone will realise it isn't a piece of bread there, but
the Christ.

59

When it was already light, there stood Jesus on the shore, though the disciples did not realise that it was Jesus. Jesus called out, 'Haven't you caught anything, friends?' And when they answered, 'No', he said, 'Throw the net out to starboard and you'll find something.' So they threw the net out and could not haul it in because of the quantity of fish. The disciple whom Jesus loved said to Peter, 'It is the Lord.' At these words, 'It is the Lord,' Simon Peter tied his outer garment round him (for he had nothing on) and jumped into the water. The other disciples came on in the boat, towing the net with the fish; they were only about a hundred yards from land.

As soon as they came ashore they saw that there was some bread there and a charcoal fire with fish cooking on it. Jesus said, 'Bring some of the fish you have just caught.' Simon Peter went aboard and dragged the net ashore, full of big fish, one hundred and fifty-three of them; and in spite of there being so many the net was not broken. Jesus said to them, 'Come and have breakfast.' None of the disciples was bold enough to ask, 'Who are you?' They knew quite well it was the Lord. (John 21:4–12)

I like these little details: the Lord had already lit the fire, ready to cook the fish. The Lord is just as considerate after his resurrection as before . . . I love God's delicacy of touch.

And another detail: after Jesus died, after Jesus was dead, here's Peter, supposed to be the prince of the apostles, the first pope – naked, trying to fish! I love the simplicity of it.

Why have we made things so complicated? Why haven't we stayed simple like Christ and his disciples?

It isn't only the pope's fault, it's much more our own fault, if the pope can't be simple like Peter. We bishops, we Christians are mainly responsible for this. It's terribly hard being pope. One day Pope John said to me, 'Oh, yes, this needs doing. That needs doing. . .' Then he went on, 'But I shan't be able to get it done.' – 'But, Father, I've been taught since I was so high that the pope has the power to do anything.' – 'Huh! If you were in my shoes, you'd know I've got eight people telling me what *not* to do.' There you have it: we tell the popes what *not* to do. If we encouraged them instead, they would take simplicity even further, which is what they want to do. I'm sure this is what they want to do. But it isn't easily done. We must do what we can to liberate the pope, liberate the bishops, liberate Christ's Church.

And the Gospel goes on to tell how Christ did with Peter what he loves doing with us too. He still asks us the same question: 'Do you love me?' The first time we hear it, our hearts quake with joy, with bliss. Then the Lord insists, 'Do you really love me?' The reason why he repeats the question a third time is because he knows how weak we are. Because of our weakness, he knows we may even be capable of wanting to offend him. He wants to preserve us from that.

And then, addressed to Peter, comes the warning Christ addresses to us all: 'When you were young, you used to put on your own belt and go where you wanted to go; but when you are old, you will stretch out your hands, and someone else will put a belt round you and take you where you won't want to go.'

Next to the grace of a good death, the most important one perhaps is that of growing old well. It's no joke growing old. But if we could, with the Lord's grace, grow old on the outside without growing old on the inside, staying young, retaining hope. . . For we have a thousand reasons for living. . .

Often I say to my doctor friends, 'You ought to invent a pill – not like the one we all know about – a pink one or a blue one which, even when our arteries are rock solid, would let us see the world as it really is: near God, in his light.'

Oh, how generous the earth is! We trample on her all

through our lives and yet she forever opens to feed us. And one day, like a mother, she will open to receive us into her womb while we await our resurrection.

60

Then he took them out as far as the outskirts of Bethany, and raising his hands he blessed them. Now as he blessed them, he withdrew from them and was carried up to heaven. They worshipped him and then went back to Jerusalem full of joy; and they were continually in the Temple praising God. (Luke 24:50–3)

What joy to know and experience this profound truth: he has left us, he has stayed behind. . . He has truly gone to the Father, he as truly is still here with us, and not solely in the Blessed Sacrament.

How do you understand the mission entrusted by Christ to his apostles? At some periods in the Church's history the mission has been discharged in ways that wouldn't be acceptable today.

You know, every age has its own pattern of life and its own way of seeing things. It isn't fair to judge the past by the way we see things today.

Admittedly, in the colonial era, the missionaries frequently arrived under the shadow of the conquerors' flag. And it was thought that what had succeeded in more developed countries would be the right system to impose. Why attempt any new experiments? What after all could be expected of these pathetic people, fit only to be pitied and be loved? With our systems, all problems were solved. And with the funds generously subscribed by the Christians who had sent us, we were able to build big schools, even universities, hospitals, leper-colonies, churches, magnificent churches. . .

Today we are no better, no wiser, no more humane, but our vision is different. And, without passing judgement, I believe ours to be closer to the Gospel even so.

When we arrive now, we know that although we have to teach – and teach is what we have to do – we have still more to learn, even from the lowliest of the lowly. For the Lord hasn't been waiting for us to arrive. He got here first. The Spirit of God was here already.

We have made what seems a very modest discovery but is a vastly important one nonetheless: it's no good only working for the people, you have to work with the people too. The essential thing is to make our brothers and sisters realise they are not things, not objects, not sub-human, but children of God with brains to think for themselves.

When visitors come to see us, they want to be shown what we're doing. In the old days there was nothing easier; we had churches, schools and hospitals to show them. Today the effects of our toil are invisible, they're so humble. . .

In Brazil, as elsewhere in Latin America, one meets priests from all over the world. They live as the humblest people do. So do the nuns. They dress like everybody else. They work like everybody else. Are people really aware of their presence? Do they really feel they're on their side?

Yes, they're deeply loved, like brothers and sisters. They aren't foreigners, since they come in the spirit of the Incarnation. Naturally, the French, the Dutch, the Swiss, the Canadians retain the characteristics of their land of birth. It isn't a matter of chance that one's been born in one country rather than another. However, while retaining these characteristics, they pass everywhere as brothers and sisters. They come to help make religion not an alien, alienating force but a force for hope.

We're all foreigners, you know, when it comes to wanting to be with the people. I too have had to learn.

Today, by God's grace, I know how to talk to my people. But I've had to learn. We're all foreigners. We're here on earth, but this isn't our home. We're pilgrims, pilgrims of the absolute, marching towards the Father's house.

152

Table of Gospel Readings